Teaching Terrific Threes
and Other Toddlers

Other Quality Early Childhood Education Titles by Terry Graham Published by Humanics Learning

Teaching Terrific Two's and Other Toddlers

Fingerplays and Rhymes for Always and Sometimes

Listening is A Way of Loving

Teaching the Terrific Threes

And Other Toddlers

A Resource Guide for the Parents, Teachers, and Care Givers of Three Year Olds

Written by
Terry Lynne Graham, M.A.

Illustrated by Nancy Clark

HUMANICS LEARNING
P.O. Box 7400
Atlanta, Georgia 30357

HUMANICS LEARNING
P.O. Box 7400
Atlanta, Georgia 30357

Illustrations by Nancy Clark
Cover Design by Jackie Kerr

First Printing 1998
Copyright 1997 Humanics Limited

Printed in the United States of America

Library of Congress Cataloging-in-Publication Data

Graham, Terry Lynn, 1949-
        Teaching terrific three's and other toddlers.
1.Toddlers—United States. 2. Day care centers—United States—Activity programs.
3.Education, Preschool—United States—Activity Programs.

ISBN: 0-89334-260-2

Acknowledgements

Thanks to all the children I have worked with and who have left a lasting impression on me- to my parents, who instilled in me a love of reading and writing. Thanks to the teachers I have worked with who have shared their ideas and supported mine. And thanks to my family, who is proud to have a teacher and an author in the family.

Dedication

ONE MORE TIME...

When you wonder why you do it,
Day, after day, after day,
And how you're going to stick to it,
Considering the hours and the pay,

Think of the children you're teaching,
Their smiles and desire to learn.
Don't jump back in bed and roll over-
You've been given a gift to return.

Who else can say they get pictures,
All original fine works of art?
Who else can say they're hugged daily,
Or get to tell 25 threes that they're smart?

Who else can heal boo-boos and owies,
Without getting a medical degree?
Who else can stand behind children,
And see the world the way it should be?

So teachers, just when you are doubting
The path you have chosen to go,
Hear your heart, not your head, and get going.
Your garden has started to grow!

Table of Contents

Cozy Spaces, Special Places
Where Can I Go?

Block Area
What Can I Build?

Dip, Dive, and Dig
Is It Ok to Splash?

Once A Pound of Time
What Does This Say?

Catch the Creative Spirit
What Can I Do?

Let's Cook
What Smells Good?

On Beyond, "What Color is This?"
What Can I Think?

Threes Outdoors
Watch Me! Watch Me!

Transitions
How Do I Get From Here to There?

Introduction

It's been 13 years since *Teaching Terrific Two's* was published and it had never occurred to me that there should be a sequel. When Humanics Ltd. approached me, somewhat apprehensively, I think they were pleasantly surprised when I enthusiastically said, "Yes!" It was time to write again and after surveying teachers and parents, I was assured that such a resource was needed.

Every age is unique unto itself. Every age is also bits and pieces of those months and years before and after. So this book is bits and pieces of years of experiences with workshop presentations, children of all ages, and the many resources I have filed away, perhaps with the idea that there *was* another book inside me left to write.

Three Year Olds....

Like for friends to come and play,
But still want things their own way.
Sometimes chunky, very spunky,
Would like to share, but not quite there.

Curious, humorous, want to know,
How things work and where things grow.
Love to learn, but not wait their turn.
Question when and where and how,
But when they want it, they want it NOW!

Big and little muscles,
That have just begun to grow,
Aren't always ready,
To write or skip or throw.

Children who were toddlers
Only yesterday,
Are ready to be "Big Kids" now
To color, cut, and play.

The classroom is their playground.
Teachers are the key.
Take them now from terrific twos,
To the joys of being THREE!

Proud Points to Ponder

Activities with the ♥ icon designate **Family** participation. Projects to take home and share with parents, brothers and sisters, or other care givers ensure that everyone the child comes in contact with has a part in the educational process. Making the school/home connections enhances family literacy goals and creates the increasingly important home to school link .

The ✸ icon indicates an **Activity** that may be modified, some materials adapted, or additional supervision may be needed in order for this activity to be appropriate for children with various special needs or a wide range of abilities.

When planning to use the activities in this book, think about how each one could be used to **strengthen**, **extend**, or **challenge** the skills and abilities of the children you teach. These activities are designed for different levels of children. You, the teacher, will apply your expertise, your intuition, and your knowledge of individual students to create an appropriate child-activity match.

Guidelines For Developmentally Appropriate Learning Environments

- All learning takes place *inside* the total child.
- Learning is what the child does, not what is done *to* the child.
- A child learns through play.
- A child learns many things at a time. Curriculum choices and teaching should reflect this.
- The child's developmental level and readiness determine activities and approaches used in the classroom.
- We use the child's interests as a vehicle for planning activities and themes. Our choices should be meaningful to the child.
- Real materials and concrete experiences create the natural learning modality.
- A variety of experiences that meet the needs of children with wide ranges of abilities are used to teach basic skills.
- Create an atmosphere of *structured freedom*, where trust promotes problem solving, thinking, initiative, and self-reliance.
- Each child is unique. Teaching should reflect this.
- Teachers are decision makers who observe, facilitate, analyze, and evaluate while continuing their own learning: learning is a life-long process.

All About Threes
What Do We Look Like, Inside and Out?

So many thoughts and feelings, inside of me to say,
Why and how, and which one?
I'm learning every day.
The whole wide world's exciting,
Everything is new.
I try to learn and listen,
But I <u>really</u> need to <u>DO!</u>

Characteristics of the Three-Year-Old Child

<u>Physical</u> : We...
...still have some of our "toddler" look.
...are beginning to cut on a straight line.
...can glue or paste but lack some control.
...can scribble.
...can hop on one foot twice or more.
...have better body control - walking, jumping, and running come easier.
...can take apart/put together.
...can even string beads!
...know how to unbutton and unzip.
...can stir and spread.

<u>Social/Emotional</u> : We...
...have some common fears.
...play in groups but do not always cooperate.
...can dress without much supervision but have our own inner time clock about how
     soon this needs to get accomplished.
...are interested in friendships.
...want to do grown-up things.
...have imaginary friends and a great imagination!

<u>Cognitive</u> : We...
...can make simple comparisons
...can do simple puzzles
...understand spatial relationships
...match and classify by color, shape, size

<u>Language</u> : We...
...have good command of vocabulary.
...speak in sentences of 4-6 words.
...are still developing some speech sounds.
...like nursery rhymes, songs, guessing games.
...are beginning to tell stories and laugh at silly jokes or riddles.
...can say our first and last name.
...ask who, what, where, when, how questions.
...can use "I" correctly.
...enjoy trying new words.

What We Need

- **Attention**
- **Patient helpers**
- **Praise for our efforts, little criticism**
- **Someone to set limits**
- **Understanding**
- **Practice to learn control of our bodies**
- **Reassurance**
- **Ways to be successful**
- **Room to run**
- **Reasons to feel proud of self, family, and heritage**
- **A consistent routine**
- **Activities and materials that meet developmental needs**
- **To be an important part of a group**

What We Like

- **Dress-up clothes**
- **Magnifying glasses**
- **Blocks**
- **Playhouses**
- **Balls**
- **Dolls**
- **Clean-up toys**
- **Puppets**
- **Stickers**
- **Clay/playdough**
- **Stringing toys**
- **Hook-together toys**
- **Wooden or rubber cars, trucks, boats**
- **Beanbags**
- **Sand toys**
- **Duplo Bricks**
- **Tents**
- **Pop beads**
- **Lacing toys**
- **Discovery toys**
- **Toys to throw and catch**
- **Rhythm records**
- **Housekeeping Furniture**
- **Kaleidoscopes**

- **Puzzles (up to 20 pieces)**
- **Counting toys**
- **Simple games**
- **Pencils, crayons, markers**
- **Pegboards**
- **Screw toys**
- **Hiding toys**
- **Wagons, tricycles, scooters**
- **Cassettes, computer games**
- **Stuffed animals**
- **Water play toys**
- **Riding vehicles**
- **Finger-paints**

Schedules

Threes feel safe with a routine that is consistent with some room for flexibility. Days that follow with the same activities at the same times encourage children to know what comes next, and to look forward to their favorite parts of the day. There should be a balance of active and quiet, and a concentration of child centered activities with teacher directed activities. Children learn best when they make choices and decisions about the way they will spend their day.

Sample Half Day Schedule:

8:45-9:00	Getting Comfortable: Choice of quiet activities/Conversations
9:00-9:15	Circle Time: Attendance/Songs/News/Fingerplays
9:15-9:30	Child Planning: "What Would You Like To Do?"
9:30-10:30	Work Time: Children work at the centers of choice/Snack open
10:25	Transition Activity:"Clean-up time is soon.Think about how you can help."
10:30-10:45	Small Group Time: Readiness activity with adult
10:45-11:00	Music/ Movement
11:00-11:15	Recall of the day's events: "What did you do today?"
11:15-11:45	Outside
11:45-12:00	Story/Dismissal

It is helpful to post the schedule where parents and volunteers can see it.

Language Arts	Poetry	Fingerplays/ Nursery Rhymes	Math	Manipulatives
Art	Literature	Music/ Movement Songs	Science	Social Studies
Outdoor Play/ Gross Motor	Publishing	Critical Thinking/ Questioning	Drama	Cooking
Centers	Dramatic Play	Blocks	Points for Parents	Special Activities
What Else	Materials	Notes	Evaluation	Notes

Sample Child's Schedule: (Drawings communicate the schedule to the children)

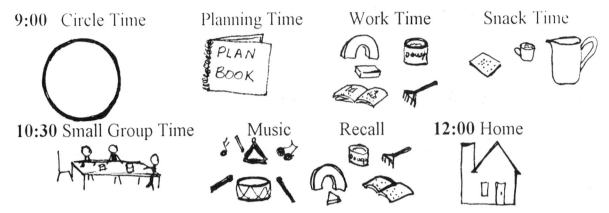

9:00 Circle Time   Planning Time   Work Time   Snack Time

10:30 Small Group Time   Music   Recall   12:00 Home

Individualizing Plans For Children

Teachers know that they must plan for of wide range of abilities in order to meet the needs of all the children in their classrooms. A helpful suggestion for making this happen is to note times on the daily schedule when individualization is to occur and designate an Individualization Block for each lesson plan. You may want to use the child's initials and a brief description of the skill you want to strengthen or challenge.

Sample Individualization Schedule

Small Group Time: Seriation (T.G./J.S)

Outdoors: Hopping (S.C.)

Checking the Environment

Teacher_____Date_____

Parent Board____

Health Board____

Equipment marked or labeled____

Cozy Corner____

Health Posters____

Multicultural Materials____
(Dolls, pictures, posters, books)

Nutrition Posters____

Art work/ Printed Materials/ Pictures at child's eye level____

Puzzles (Anti-biased)____

Assessment folders____

Socket covers____

Fire extinguisher____
(Can staff operate it?)

Toxic materials stored and locked____

Covered trash cans____

Toothbrushes stored to
prevent cross-contamination____

Attractive, busy, orderly classroom____

Staff area is inviting, clean and neat____

General safety check inside____

General safety check outside____

Learning centers defined and labeled____

Menu posted____

Emergency plans posted____

Comments:

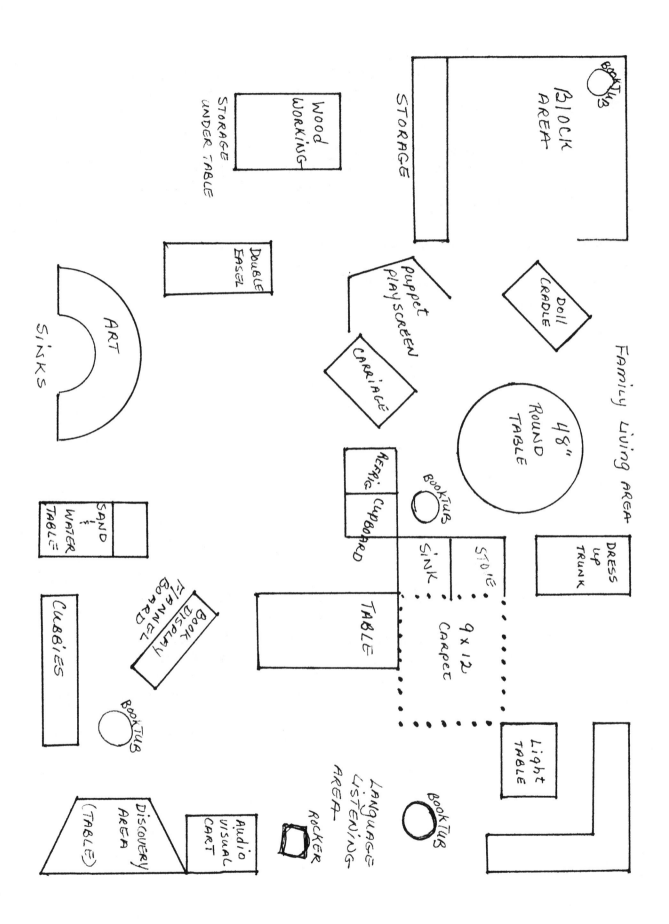

BLOCK AREA

BOOK TUB

STORAGE

Family Living Area

STORAGE UNDER TABLE

WOOD WORKING

DOUBLE EASEL

Puppet playscreen

CARRIAGE

Doll CRADLE

ART

SINKS

48" ROUND TABLE

AERIAL CUPBOARD

BOOK TUB

DRESS UP TRUNK

SAND & WATER TABLE

Book DISPLAY FLANNEL BOARD

SINK

STORE

9 × 12 CARPET

CUBBIES

TABLE

BOOK TUB

Light TABLE

Discovery AREA (TABLE)

Audio visual CART

ROCKER

LANGUAGE LISTENING AREA

BOOK TUB

Teaching Techniques

Now that you have spent untold hours organizing your classroom, reviewing the children's health records and family background, developing a tentative flexible schedule, and creating name tags, now comes the hardest part. What to teach??? A good place to start is to think about something we can all do easily- Play. Play is the work of young children and teachers are their guides. It is through play that they learn the skills for success, how to solve their own problems, communicate, and develop the ability to make decisions, as well as becoming aware of who they are and the role they will play in life. Play follows the natural process of learning by doing.

A Precious Key

How can I teach my child, I said?
And see for her what lies ahead.

I wish, in school, I'd paid more heed,
To learn the skills my child would need.

The one wish that I want to earn,
Is simply to make it fun to learn,

My child looked up with toy in hand,
She said, "Your wish is my command.

To your precious time, you hold the key,
Come on now and play with me."

Your key to what to teach should come from the children themselves. What does a three year old like to do? What excites, interests, and motivates a three year old?

As you work with your children, a curriculum begins to unfold. Vacations, special visitors, a new toy, a movie, or a pet can all be opportunities for learning. You may want to keep an on-going record of things children say and do as you observe them in their play. Their actions, imaginations, artwork, and even disagreements will help you plan for their experiences.

The world of the three year old is filled with exploration and experimentation, successes and trying agains, and learning how to learn. It is a time to be a child, to play at growing up, and have a teacher who understands all of these things.

Fingerplay Rhyme Time: Five Green Frogs

What Do I Learn?

- Language Skills

What Do I Need?

- Finger Puppets: Five Green Frogs. You can make your own finger puppets by sewing two pieces of scrap fabric together, making sure that a finger will fit inside, and drawing a face on one side. Ears and tails made out of small pieces of fabric or paper can be glued or sewn on. If you have an old pair of gloves, just cut the fingers off and you have ready-made finger puppets who only need some decoration to be a big hit!

What Do I Do?

Sing or chant the fingerplay rhymes.

Five Green Frogs

Five green frogs jumped in the pool.
The first frog said, "Wow, this is cool!"
The second frog said, "Too cool for me!"
"I'm hopping out!" said number three.
The fourth frog swam, then took a dive,
While "Ribbet! Ribbet! Ribbet!" croaked number five.

Fingerplay Rhyme Time: Old MacDonald

What Do I Learn?

- Language Skills

What Do I Need?

- Finger Puppets: Old McDonald Had A Farm

What Do I Do?

Tune: Twinkle, Twinkle Little Star

Old McDonald Had A Farm : Riddle and Rhymes

I can peep, lay eggs and cluck. Here's a hint: I'm not a duck!
Moo, give milk, eat grass, of course. Here's a hint: I'm not a horse!
Run, and jump, and grow quite big. Here's a hint: I'm not a pig!
Oink and eat, I'm quite a hog. Here's a hint: I'm not a dog!

What Else?

Make copies of the following patterns, cut each animal out, color, laminate, and glue to popsicle sticks or tongue depressors. Distribute to the class and ask the children to stand up when their animal is the answer to the riddle. This activity fits in well with the Critical Thinking Strategies discussed later in the book.

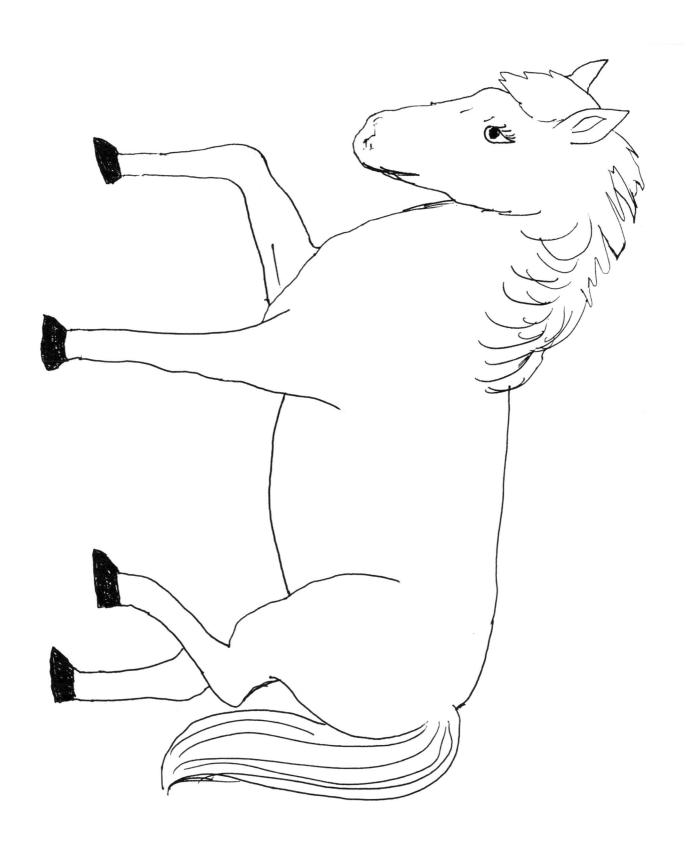

Fingerplay Rhyme Time:
Ten Little Children of the World

What Do I Learn?
- Language Skills

What Do I Need?
- Finger Puppets: Ten Little Children of the World

What Do I Do?
Tune: Twinkle, Twinkle Little Star

Ten Little Children of the World

Ten little children from the world around,
Some are white, some black or brown.
We come from cities and we come from town.
Ten little children from the world around.

Ten little children from far away lands,
Play in the seas and desert sands.
We all look different from these different parts,
We're ten little children with loving hearts.

Fingerplay Rhyme Time: Ten Little Gardeners

What Do I Learn?

- Language Skills

What Do I Need?

- Finger Puppets: Ten Little Gardeners

What Do I Do?

Chant the fingerplay as the children take turns with the puppets.

Ten Little Gardeners

The first little Gardener went to plant a tree.
The second little Gardener said, "Wait for me."
The third one said, "Let's go together."
The fourth one said, "We'll need good weather."
The fifth one said, "Rain will make it grow."
The sixth one said, "I'll bring the hoe."
The seventh one said, "We'll hope for sun."
The eighth one said, "This is fun!"
The ninth one said, "How long will it take?"
The tenth one said, "I'll bring a rake."
The ten little Gardeners worked for hours.
The next time they said, "Let's just plant flowers!"

Love in the Classroom
How Do We Get Along?

There's more to school than book learning.
There's manners and getting along.
There's more than just numbers and counting,
ABC's or singing a song.
There's respect and love for your neighbor,
There's making and being a friend.
There's knowing the joys of just learning,
And it's that love that must never end.

Management and Discipline

You can manage your classroom. You can set up learning areas and special places, and equip these areas with appropriate, exciting, and creative materials. You can develop a daily routine, with alternating active/quiet experiences, allowing for times children make choices and times for teacher directed experiences. A balance of both is the key. But manage children? Here the key is to be pro-active and teach them to manage their own behavior. We can do that with a little imagination, a little creativity, and lots of love.

The three year old is developing strong language skills by this time and enjoys experimenting and role playing. This makes using puppets or stuffed animals a natural approach to creating good behavior. The following puppets are a few examples; the collection can be easily extended.

Tips While Using Puppets

Try not to gender type the puppets. Whenever possible, use the puppet's name instead of assigning a gender and avoid saying, "He doesn't share" or "She is a good friend".
The puppets never physically fight.

Bringing About Better Behavior Puppet and Stuffed Animal Collection
Any puppet or stuffed animal can be turned into a good behavior teaching tool.
Here are a few suggestions.

I Love Ewe (Lamb)
Possibly the most important member of this puppet family, I Love Ewe handles all kinds of situations. She tells the children everyday that she loves them and she teaches the universal sign for "I love you". I Love Ewe also encourages children to express their feelings to each other, to their families, and to the other adults who care for them. I Love Ewe interacts with the other puppets and teaches them to solve problems.

Sel-Fish (Fish)
Sel-Fish has not learned to share or is not developmentally ready to give what he's got to someone else. Pair Sel-Fish up with Share Bear and let Share Bear explain why friends share and some other ways to make sure everyone has a turn.

Share Bear (Teddy Bear)
Share Bear talks to the class when he sees children in the act of sharing materials. He may say, "I saw Tanya and Koffi sharing the big blocks. They were having a good time together." After clean-up Share Bear may re-cap work time by highlighting good "sharers".

Mooove Over Moo Cow (Cow)

When a child's personal space is infringed upon, Moo Cow reminds everyone that it helps if we all just Mooove Over! The puppet doesn't even have to talk. Its appearance means "Mooove Over."

Cryin' Lion (Lion)

Teachers should always be the primary comforters when a child is distressed. Sometimes there isn't time to give individual attention, and that's where Cryin' Lion does his job. Make this puppet accessible so that the children can get the puppet out and tell him what has made them unhappy. Older children can "write" their feelings down and leave their letters for Cryin' Lion to answer later.

It's Mine Mina Bird (Crow, parrot)

This puppet needs to make friends with Share Bear. Teachers can ask, "Did we hear any It's Mine Mina Birds in our class today?"

Wordswork Walrus (Walrus)

We solve our problems with words, never physically. Wordswork gives children examples of how words work. Teachers can tell children to say, "I don't like that!" instead of physically hurting others.

Clean Up King & Queen (Elephants)

This dynamic duo lets everyone know how much play time is left and when clean up time will begin. They work together. They watch for good "cleaner-uppers" and they announce the names to the class.

Tattling Tiger (Tiger)

There are several reasons for tattling; attention getting, recognition, low self-esteem, or lack of social skill development, among others. There are times when children need to "report." Know the difference between a child who tattles for attention and one who is relating a real problem. A child who tattles for attention may be referred to Tattling Tiger. Tell your "news" to this understanding, good listening puppet.

Peaceful Pig (Pig)

Our calming, transitional friend. Peaceful Pig makes an appearance when it's time to rest or change activities quietly. Peaceful also reports on children who have proven to be peacemakers.

Husha Bunny (Rabbit)

Husha Bunny and Peaceful Pig make good friends. Husha Bunny's job is to get those little ones ready to hear a story, listen to a special visitor, or walk out for a fire drill. This puppet does not speak. When Husha appears, everyone gets very quiet.

Helpful Hippo (Hippopotamus)

Helpful Hippo lives up to his name. He is always ready to lend a hand, clean up willingly, and think of ways to help others.

Friendly Fox (Fox)

Finally, a fox who's a good character. Friendly Fox has a very important role in the classroom. This puppet describes the attributes of friendship so that children learn what friends do and what it means to be a friend. "Friends share. Friends don't hit.

Friends help each other. Friends say nice things to each other." Friendly Fox could teach Sel-Fish a lesson.

Patient Porpoise (Porpoise)
Soothe those "Me firsters" and children who have a difficult time waiting their turn. Patient Porpoise tells the good things about being last, such as the caboose guiding and balancing the whole train. Sometimes the line of children gets reversed and those who were first are now last! Patient Porpoise also appears to give a "Patient Person Presentation." That's a list of children who were patient today.

Manners the Monkey (Monkey)
More than *please* and *thank you*, Manners the Monkey knows that when we use good manners we show respect for ourselves and others.

Make It Better Butterfly (Butterfly)
Teachers and parents are the best comforters but sometimes a butterfly kiss can take away the pain as well.

Books Can Help

- *Mail Myself To You* by Woodie Gutherie (Good Year Books)

- *Rude Giants* by Audrey Wood (Harcourt Brace)

- *The Thingamajigs Book of Manners* by Dick Keller (Children's Ideal)

- *I Can Share* by Bonnie Worth (Muppet Press)

- *Richard Scarry's Please and Thank You Book* by Richard Scarry (Random House)

- *The Kissing Hand* by Audrey Penn (Child Welfare League)

- *Peace Begins With You* by Katherine Scholes (Little Brown and Co.)

Learning to Cooperate

Threes are still very independent workers but they are beginning to enjoy group activities and can experience small group or partnered activities. To encourage cooperation, use some of these activities at small group time.

1. "It's My Turn" Name Box

Create 2 boxes, one for names and one for activities. Write everyone's name on a card. Place the name cards in the name box. Write several activities on cards (i.e. do a puzzle, build a tower, cook a dinner) and place the cards in the activity box. Draw 2 names. Let the 2 children draw from the activity box or decide on a task they choose to do together.

2. Where Are My Kitties?

A variation of Hide and Seek. One child hides, while everyone else looks. When another child finds the hidden child, they hide together. Whenever the children hiding are found, the "seekers" join them in their hiding place. That's cooperation

3. Cooperation Fruit Salad

Plan: Everyone thinks of a fruit. Ask the children to bring in the fruit from home. Record the fruits on a chart. Post the chart in the room. Bring some extra fruit for children who are unable to contribute.

Cooperation Fruit Salad

- Wash Fruit.
- Chop the big fruit into little pieces.
- Add all fruit to big bowl.
- Add 1 cup plain yogurt and stir.
- Serve in small cup with spoons.

4. A Hunting We Will Go

Threes love to hunt for things. Pull 2 names out of the box to put partners together. Give the partners bags or baskets. Hide cottonballs, feathers, plastic fruits or items that extend a theme (i.e. small cars or trucks for a transportation theme). Encourage the partners to work together to find the objects.

5. Tug of Peace

Children sit in groups of four around a large plastic hoop. They place their hands on the hoop and on the count of three, they all try to stand up. Encourage helping each other.

Taking Turns and Sharing

Toddler's Creed

If I want it, it's mine
If I give it to you and change my mind later,
It's still mine.
If I can take it away from you, it's mine.
If I had it a while ago, it's mine.
If it's mine, it will never belong to anyone else.
If we are building something together, all the pieces are mine.
If it just looks like mine, it's mine.

If sharing means taking away what I have and giving it to you, it's no wonder that sharing is a skill that threes still have not mastered. To encourage three year olds to get past the "It's Mine" stage, the following suggestions may be helpful:

1. My Turn- Your Turn
Write each child's name on a 3x5 note card and place the cards on a metal ring. Whose turn is it to be the leader, to use a new toy, or select a song to sing? Just look at the name on the card. This also lets the children know who will get to be first the next time.

2. Timing Toys
There will always be toys that everyone wants to play with, usually all at the same time. Place a kitchen timer or hour glass in the block area. Show the children how to set the timers for each other. Give up the toy when your time is over.

3.   A Musical Signal
Use a tambourine or drum beat as a signal for giving a popular toy to someone else. Be sure to use your Share Bear puppet to talk about those children who willingly shared.

4. Coloring Share Bear
Share Bear says, "We Share". Give the children bear patterns to color. Write their names on each one. Create a bulletin board for displaying the bears, representing good sharers in the classroom.

5. Share Bear's Song
Tune: Way Down Yonder in the Paw Paw Patch

I like the way that____ is sharing
      (child's name)

I like the way that____ is sharing.
      (child's name)

I like the way that ____ is sharing.
      (child's name)

Good friends like to share.

Making the Classroom Fit for Threes

Good behavior and classroom design and daily routine go together. A developmentally appropriate environment, with materials that inspire, challenge, and motivate, creates a place for children to grow. Behavior problems are kept at a minimum. Keep these suggestions handy for creating a place for three year olds.

Threes say;

- We like shelves and tables at the right height (approx. 18 inches).
- We like clear containers filled with toys or art materials for making our choices easier.
- We need space that's uncluttered, cause we still have our clumsy moments.
- We need space to "get away from it all"; a special place to be mad, alone, or get it back together.
- We like times to play alone, with others, and in small groups. Big groups are hard 'cause we are just learning to share or listen, and still need lots of individual attention from our teachers.
- We need active <u>and</u> quiet times.
- We need lots of choices, but we need to have some things we <u>have</u> to do. That prepares us for life.
- We like routine. We don't handle big changes well. Let us know when our daily routine will be different.
- We threes are becoming learners. Give us lots to learn and lots of ways to learn it. We are developing our own learning styles.
- We threes are often part twos, part threes, and part fours. Tailor our activities and toys to meet a variety of levels.

Laugh with us. Love with us. We are barely more than 1000 days old.
We have so far to go.

Kissing Hands

What Do I Learn?
- Care for Others
- Fine Motor Skills
- Language Skills

What Do I Need?
- *The Kissing Hand* by Audrey Penn
- Construction Paper
- Heart stickers or stamps
- Crayons
- Scissors

What Do I Do?
Read the story of Chester the raccoon and *The Kissing Hand.*
"Can you trace around your hand onto the paper? Now someone will help you cut it out. Put a heart sticker or stamp in the palm of the hand Maybe you can even draw a heart."

What Else?
Talk about the story.
"If you met Chester, what would you say? Have you ever felt the way Chester felt when he went off to school?"
To cut your own heart shape, use the following pattern.

Teachers: End your day by giving each child a heart sticker.

Nap Happy

Sometimes nap or rest time can be a stressful time for children and teachers. Here are some suggestions for helping children adapt to and enjoy this part of their day.

1. Napping Wands

Create a Napping Wand by gluing some soft feathers to a paper towel roll. Choose a different child each day who gets the chance to wake the other children with a touch or tickle from the Napping Wand.

2. Readers

Always allow children who do not sleep to get some books, paper, pencils, or crayons to keep them occupied. Small flashlights are available for these avid readers.

3. Comforters

Some threes get teary at nap time. Ask parents to send stuffed animals or family photographs for the child to hold onto during rest. These items can be very comforting.

4. Gentle Touch

While the children are resting, walk around the room and rub their backs or touch fingers, backs, or feet with a soft paint brush. "Keep your eyes closed and tell me what part of you I'm touching".

5. Resting Puppet Pals

Designate one puppet to be a Puppet Pal. This puppet goes on a nap walk each day and talks to each child, comforting them or wishing them a pleasant rest.

6. Nap Conductors

Rest time is the perfect time to introduce classical music. Experiment with the Pier Gynt Suite or Beethoven's Pastorale. Use the name box to assign different children to select the music to be played at naptime.

7. Napping Partners

Allow two "friends" to rest together in a special place in the room that they have chosen.

8. "Get Up Sleepy Head"

Have one child draw names from the name box each day to announce whose turn it is to get up and put their cot away.

Napping Themes

Integrate Nap Time with the themes you teach.

1. The Sea: Encourage the children to bring beach towels to rest on; play a cassette of ocean waves. You could also hang a beach mural along the base of the wall.

2. The Seasons: Place calendar pictures along the base of the wall where the children can see them while resting.

3. Shelters, Habitats, and Homes: Help the children drape blankets or towels over tables to create a fort, tent, or different kind of place to sleep (see next theme).

4. Farm, Woods, or Jungle: Create an environmental mural with crayons or markers on several large sheets. Allow the children to place their cots or rest mats **in** the jungle, farm, or woods.

5. Time and Number: Give the early risers a rainbow gummed chain link to add to a Nap Chain. Count them each day.

Nap Surprises

Hide a surprise under each "Good Rester's" cot. Threes love to hunt for things, and especially like to be pleasantly surprised.

Seasonal Surprises

Thanksgiving: A feather to be made into a class turkey after rest time.

Winter: Three white circles to be made into a snowman.

Valentine's Day: A construction paper heart or foil-wrapped candy.

St. Patrick's Day: Tie a green ribbon on the "Best Resters of the Day" cots.

Easter: A plastic colored egg

Birthdays: A card made and "signed" by all the children.

Stories: Hide felt board pieces under some children's cots. Use the pieces to tell a story after rest time.

Napping Times Napping Rhymes

Dollie

When it's time to take a nap,
I hold my dollie in my lap,
And sing to him of days gone by
And whisper "Hush," if he should cry.
Then when it's time for nap to end,
I snack with dollie and a friend.

Cot Topics

Rest time is the time for me
To sneak my book where she can't see
And quietly turn the well- worn pages
For what must seem to others like ages
But there's never enough time to look,
When you share nap time with a book.

A Rude Awakening

Rest Time
Quiet Time
Shadows and breezes
But everyone laughs when somebody sneezes!

Nap Mats

Do you like to take a rest?
It's the part that I like best.
I snuggle on my bright blue mat
And for awhile imagine that,
I'm on a flying carpet high overhead,
Exploring places while in bed

Teacher's Nap Time

My teacher thinks that we're asleep.
My eyes are open, just a peep.
She writes and plans in her big blue book,
Cuts out circles, then takes a look
To see if each of us is well
To rub our backs or secrets tell.
She listens for a quiet cry,
She never sits, I wonder why.
She's busy doing what she does best,
But when do teachers get to rest?

Turning *Me* into *We*
Do I Have To Share?

Long ago when I was one,
I was the center, like the sun.
Then long ago when I was two,
I wanted to do what I chose to do.
But now that I'm a grown-up three,
I'm beginning to like the sound of WE!

Friendly Threes

What Do I Learn?
- Friendships
- Celebrating Diversity
- Creativity
- Fine Motor Skills
- Positive Self-Image

What Do I Need?
- *Friends at School* by Rochelle Bunnett
- Tag Board Pre-cut Frames
- Stickers
- Crayons
- Glue

What Do I Do?
Read the story about the friends you can meet at school.
"Draw a picture of a friend you have at your school. Maybe you have many special friends. Now let teacher put your picture in the frame. You can color or add stickers to your frame."

What Else?
Add those framed works of art to a **Friendship Art Gallery.**

Draw a picture of yourself and frame it! Decorate the frame and place the framed works of art on an Art Gallery Bulletin Board or in an "I Am Special" Art Gallery.

 **Friendship Murals**

What Do I Learn?
- Fine Motor Skills
- Making Predictions
- Language Skills
- Positive Self-Image

What Do I Need?
- Child Shaped Stencil
- Mural Paper
- Tape
- Large Crayons with Paper Removed

What Do I Do?

Show the children the child stencils. Now tape several of them to a table top and cover with mural paper. Give the children crayons and show them how to "rub" over the stencils to make them appear. "Which child is you? Can you add a face? Clothes?" As the stencil begins to appear, ask, "What do you think the picture will be?" As the child finishes coloring ask, "Which person on our mural is most like you?"

What Else?

Give each child a child shape to decorate and take home. Use this cut out to trace all the family members. Place them on the **Family Refrigerator Art Gallery.**

Reach Out and Touch Someone **Books**

Trace 5 stencils on felt sheets and then cut them out. Glue them to tag board, one on each page, to create a book. Punch holes and add metal rings to the tag board. Ask the children to dictate the text.

The Mirror

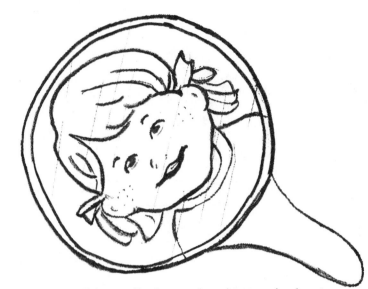

What Do I Learn?
- Body Parts
- Positive Self-Image
- Language Skills

What Do I Need?
- Hand Mirrors
- Full-length mirror
- Mirror Pattern
- Foil
- Tagboard

What Do I Do?

Here's a small group activity to help children talk about what they see in the mirror. Give each child a hand mirror, or have 3-4 sit in front of a table mirror.

"Point to the place on your face that helps you see/hear/smell. What color is your hair? Who has hair that is the same color? Skin that is the same color?"

Make a mirror for every child, using the following pattern. Give the children a piece of foil to cover the mirror.

What Else?

Copy the poem and glue it to the back of the mirror. Put a copy of the poem on the full length mirror in the dramatic play center.

Who's that with a happy face?
Feelin' good, all hairs in place?
Who's that with hands washed and clean?
Smilin' big and bold and mean?
Who's that with teeth brushed each day,
With body strong for work and play?
Who's that with a heart (insert a heart shape) of gold?
It must be my favorite Three Year Old!

 **Watch Me Grow**

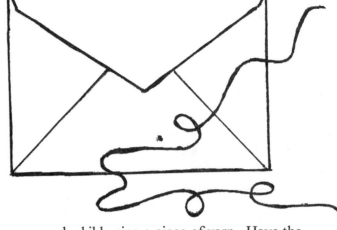

What Do I Learn?
- Language Skills
- Comparisons
- Positive Self Image

What Do I Need?
- Yarn
- Envelope
- Scissors

What Do I Do?
At the beginning of the year, measure each child using a piece of yarn. Have the child hold the yarn on top of her head and cut it at her feet. Place the yarn in an envelope with the child's name, symbol, and the date of the measurement. At the end of the year, repeat the activity and compare the lengths of yarn. Send the envelope home to share with parents.

What Else?
Copy this poem and glue it to the envelope:

Look how much I've grown this year!
I used to be this,
And now I'm here!
I was big, but I'll soon turn four,
So to measure with yarn,
We'll need lots more!

 # "We" People

What Do I Learn?
- Me Into We
- Cooperation

What Do I Need?
- Crayons or Markers
- People Patterns

What Do I Do?
Give a people pattern to each table of children (use the following patterns). Tell them that we will make a person that is a part of all of us. Tell the first child to make the pattern look like a person until you say STOP. Then pass the pattern to the next child. Put the Finished People on a "WE" bulletin board.

What Else?
Give each child a pattern to decorate as himself. These can be taken home to share with family.

Just Feelin' Good

Here are some suggestions for helping children feel good about themselves. Those children who have positive self concepts are more likely to be successful in school.

- **Special:** Go to an office supply store and have an "I AM SPECIAL" stamp made. Use the stamp for badges, art work or awards.

- **Leader:** Choose a "Child of the Day". This child gets to be the leader or messenger. The other children tell what they like about this special person.

- **Song:** Sing this song to your "Child of the Day."
    I like_____she's our special girl.
        (Name)
    She's her mommy and daddy's precious pearl.

    I like_____he's our special boy.
        (Name)
    He's his mommy and daddy's pride and joy.

- **Personality:** Practice saying good things about your students that have nothing to do with the way they look. "I like the way you share. It makes me happy when you help each other. Friends help each other. The class did such a good job today." Children have control of their actions, but very little control over their personal appearance.

50

Sing Me A Song

Song: I Am Special
Tune: Are You Sleeping?

I am special, I am special,
If you look, you will see,
Someone very special,
Someone very special,
Yes it's me. Yes, it's me!

Song: I Like You
Tune: GGE GGE GAGEFG FFD FED GAGEDC

I like you
I like you.
I hope that you like me.
I like you .
I like you.
That's very plain to see!

Song: I Am Me
Tune: EDEC EDEC EDECD CDC EFE GAGFEDC

Me!
Me -Me- Me- Me- Me- Me- Me- Me- Me- Me!
I am ME. (Point to self)
I am ME.
I am _____ for all to see!
     (Name)

Self-Portrait Class Books

What Do I Learn?
- Me Into We
- Positive Self-Image

What Do I Need?
- Tagboard
- Metal Rings
- Crayons or Markers
- Hole Punch

What Do I Do?
Each child draws her self-portrait, teachers and assistants too! Punch 2 holes at the top and add the metal rings to create a flip book. Add each child's name at the top. Read the book with the same text as *Brown Bear, Brown Bear*.

Mrs. Graham, Mrs., Graham, what do you see?
I see Danny looking at me.
Danny, Danny, what do you see?
I see Tasha looking at me.
Tasha, Tasha, what do you see?
I see Sam looking at me.

What Else?
Read: *Brown Bear, Brown Bear* by Eric Carl

Introducing...Me!

What Do I Learn?
- Language Skills
- Positive Self-Image
- Memory

What Do I Need?
- Paper Bag
- People Shape
- Crayons or Markers
- Glue

What Do I Do?
Give each child a person pattern to decorate (use the child stencils from this book). "Can you make it look like you? What color hair and eyes do you have?" Help the children glue the shapes to their paper bags. Tell the children to take the bags home and put in some of their favorite things. Bring the bags back to school. Use the bags at "Show and Tell" time. Choose a bag each day. Can the class guess whose bag it is? Let each child tell about the things inside.

What Else?
Use the bags again. Show an item from one of the bags. Can the children remember who brought it? Show another bag. "This is Carlotta's bag. Who can tell me something that Carlotta brought?"

Did Everyone Get A Chance to Be Smart Today?

There are 8 different kinds of intelligence. To make sure children get to shine in their particular area, use the following checklist as you plan and teach.

<u>Intelligence Checklist</u>

Verbal___

Math and Logic___

Spatial___

Physical___

Artistic____

Musical___

Social___

Emotional___

Recreate this sign to post near your classroom door:

<u>Teacher,</u>
**Did you reach
Each child today?
With your eyes?
With your words?
With your hands?
With your heart?**

For once they pass through your door, you may never have this chance again.

Cozy Spaces, Special Places
Where Can I Go?

Here's a place that I can go,
Where I can let my feelings show.
No one will tell me what to do,
Or make me talk if I don't want to.
Where I can sit and dream awhile,
And when I'm ready, come out and smile.

Cozy Spaces, Special Places

Everyone, adults and children alike, needs a getaway place. The busy classroom, as well as the rough and tumble playground, should include the 4 R's: spaces to **re**group, **re**lax, and **re**turn to mainstream activity, when **re**ady. Three year olds, because they are in such a unique transitional stage, will benefit emotionally and socially when the classroom environment includes a cozy place. Here are some suggestions for creating special places:

- Plan for two special spaces - one inside and one outside.
- Place the space in a protected, low traffic area of classroom or playground.
- Plan the space for no more than two children - any more and privacy is lost.

Cardboard Boxes

Remember giving a young child a gift, watching her delightedly unwrap it, then toss the gift away and play with the box? Boxes of all kinds hold a marvelous fascination for children, and very large boxes provide hours of cozy space time as well as expanding and supporting theme teaching.

- Car
- Spaceship
- Ship
- Treehouse
- Big Box
- Jungle
- Fort
- Castle
- House
- Airplane

Mazes, Tents, Cubes, Hollows, and Lofts

There are many commercially made fabric mazes and tents, sturdy plastic cubes and soft foam hollows, and large wooden lofts that can be used for cozy areas. Even a toddler-sized plastic wading pool designates an area to be used alone or shared with a friend. You may also remember as a child creating a "fort" by hanging a blanket over a card table. This idea has provided a fun place to hide for children for many generations. Make sure the blanket is secure and that you can still supervise activity.

Cozy Corners

Sometimes a rug and a few soft pillows, a basket of books, and some pictures placed at a child's eye level can be enough to create a peaceful, private place.

Materials

Let the *children* plan for things they would like to see in their special place. It's their place. Ask how they would like to decorate it. Talk about a place at home that makes them feel good. What are the things that are in that place?

- Crayons and Markers to draw windows and doors
- Tape
- Rugs
- Pillows or beanbag chairs
- Tape recorder and cassettes
- Bucket of books
- Photographs of family members
- Small, low table
- Battery powered light or lamp
- Flashlights
- Kaleidoscopes
- Stuffed animals
- Plants
- Puzzles

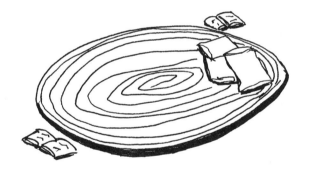

Change the materials in this area when necessary but it might be a good idea to get your three year olds prepared for the changes. They like and rely on their routines. If they go to the special place and expect to find a favorite stuffed animal friend there, it had better be there!

Quiet Bottles

1. Sparkling Water

Take an 8 oz. Plastic water bottle, remove the label, and fill it with water, a few sequins, glitter, colored plastic disks, and small shells or buttons. This makes a great therapeutic quiet toy. A little glue around the top ensures safety.

2. Bubbling Bottle

A bottle of Karo Syrup, label removed and several marbles dropped inside and the top glued back on, creates an interesting sight to observe during quiet time.

3. Shimmering Waves

Mix 2 parts mineral oil to 1 part vinegar to 2 parts water. Add a few drops blue and green food coloring. Shake!

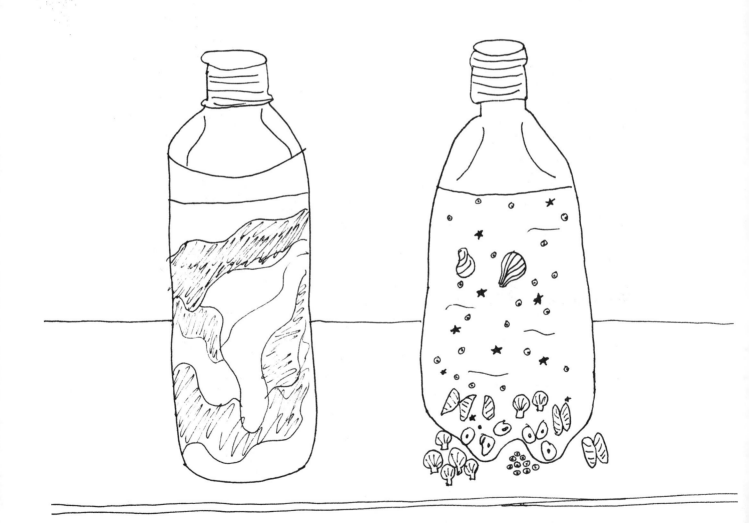

Block Area
What Can I Build?

All shapes and sizes of blocks,
Build a fortress or a town.
I hope somebody doesn't come,
To knock my tower down!

Building Problem-Solving Skills

Three year olds are becoming builders. Threes are moving from piling blocks on top of each other to making actual constructions. Roads are now leading to towers, and those towers may be surrounded by moats, fences, racetracks, and other enclosures. These creative explorers are seeing mathematical relationships through their new discoveries of enclosures. Size, shape, space and number leads them to making bridges. Now they can build up, out, and around. Block building encourages making predictions and solving problems. New trial and error learning rises and falls with those block towers every day.

The block area is fertile ground for language development - "Mine is the tallest. How high can we go?" *Biggest, More, and No!* are often sounded from one of the favorite places in the classroom. It's also a stage for social relationships to grow and the spirit of cooperative play just may begin to emerge front and center!

The three year old likes to explore and experiment with a wide variety of blocks. Unit blocks, large cardboard and wooden hollow blocks, shape blocks and chunky Duplo bricks help this new "construction worker" redesign the world.

Teachers often wonder what to do when a child chooses to play in the block area every day. Is the child missing out on other experiences and skills? This area may be providing a security for the child. Try modifying the area to meet more of the needs that he might satisfy when choosing the art area or reading corner.

"Rebuilding" Blocks

Expand the skills children need, or spark a new interest in a well-used area, by adding these materials to your block center.

- Books- Every center should have books.
- Jump Ropes/ Hoops- Build inside the circles.
- Foil/ Shiny paper
- Paper, tape and markers- Tape your name to your structure that you want to save.
- Make signs (example follows) for structures that should be left overnight.

UNDER

CONSTRUCTION

Variations:

Additions to the Block Area:
1. Outline block shapes on posterboard to create your own block puzzles.
2. Make sure a dollhouse permanently resides in the block area, and have other dolls visit frequently.
3. Supply flashlights and acrylic mirrors.
4. Add a tent or maze.
5. Place a sheet on the floor and draw a jungle, farm, or town.
6. Watch block play change.

Pose a Problem of the Day-
7. What would we do if there was a flood and the roads were washed away?
8. What would we do if we could only build with triangle blocks?

Theme Building
9. Read the *Three Little Pigs*. Put pictures of pigs, pig puppets, Easter grass, pipe stems, and large craft sticks in the block area.
What might the children build now?

Dip, Dive, and Dig
Is It OK to Splash?

Float it! Sink it! Dip it!
Be careful not to sip it!
Water, we can splash it,
And sand, we like to mash it.
A bubble, we can blow it,
But sand, don't ever throw it!

Activities at the Sand & Water Table

Threes enjoy exploring sand and water, and its the perfect opportunity to integrate science, math, language, and social skills. Before planning for any of these activities, make sure the children have had ample time to experience self-initiated play.

Have the following sign near your table to remind children, volunteers, and teachers that hand washing is an important health practice.

Did you...?

Wash your hands before water play?
Dry them and throw your towel away?

Now that you have had some fun,
Wash them again and now you're done!

Sand and Water Fun

1. Ice Cube Surprises

Save small plastic insects, colored beads, coins, or plastic flowers. Put them in an ice cube tray, add water, and freeze overnight. Place the cubes in the water table. Record your three's reactions. What happens as the ice cubes melt?

2. Seek and Find

Hide plastic letters or numbers in the bubbles or in the sand.

3. Banner Art

Laminate some of the threes' artwork. Staple or glue the pieces to jumbo craft sticks. Add these to your sand table. The children will enjoy playing with their own creations.

4. Rainbow Water

Place a few drops of food coloring in the water.

5. Bubbles

Take the water table outside for Bubble Day. Use pipestems to create bubble wands. Who can make the largest bubble? Does a square wand make a square bubble?

6. Senses

Add colored paper, cellophane, foil, or some baby powder to change the look or the scent of your table activities.

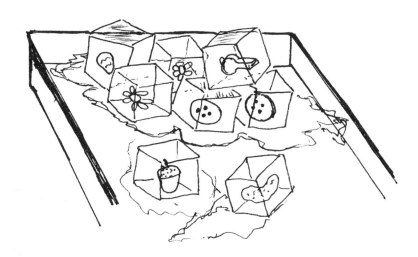

7. Sink the Boat

Place a plastic boat in the water table. Give the children some large gem clips or marbles. How many can you put in the boat before it sinks?

8. Paleontologist

Add small paint brushes and play Paleontologist or Archaeologist. Brush off bones or pieces of a dinosaur puzzle. Now put the pieces back together.

9. Integrated Play

Have poems and pictures around the sand/water area.

Sand	**Water**
Drifting, Sifting	Reflections of dew
Shovels and Sieves	In the morning light,
Castles and Dunes	Are the sunshine's petals
The ocean gives.	Dropped overnight.

10. Matching

Talk about the names of the sand/water toys used. Trace their shapes and ask the children to match the toys with their outlines.

- sieves
- funnels
- buckets
- brushes
- waterwheel
- molds
- fountains
- boats
- shovels
- cups
- spoons
- sand combs
- eggbeater

11. Sand and Story Boxes

Read the children a story like *The Three Little Pigs*. Get three shoe boxes and fill them with different story props for the children to retell the story at the sand table.

Box # 1	Box # 2	Box # 3
Easter Grass	Pipe Stems	3 Plastic dinosaurs
3 Peanuts	4 Pig cut outs	Duplo Bricks
Several craft sticks	Foil paper	Pom poms
Duplo Bricks	2 Small boxes	Jumbo craft sticks

12. Themes

Coordinate Sand and Water play with theme teaching.

Nutrition: Hide the pieces of a fruit/ vegetable or healthy meal puzzle.

Self and Family: Add Wedgie Wooden Families, Duplo Community, or World People.

Sea: Hide plastic fish, whales, and plenty of shells.

Other Treasures:

*Packing peanuts (spray with static guard to omit static) *Shredded Paper
*Easter Grass *Rice/colored Rice
*Cornstarch and Water Mixture *Beans
*Macaroni *Cotton Balls
*Add sea salt to create the 'beach' *Pom Poms

"Once A Pound of Time"
What Does This Say?

Tell me a story, read me a book.
Without pretty pictures, in my mind I must look.
One precious gift every child will need,
Is to learn to tell stories, and to make choices to read.

A young student in one of my classes turned in a story which began, "Once a pound of time." Although I'm sure she meant, "Once upon a time," I thought that her language was beautiful. This experience also made me realize how very important it is for children to learn to express themselves through writing.

Selecting Books for Three Year Olds

Threes suggest:

- Picture Books
- Fairy Tales
- Folk Tales
- Animal Stories
- Humor and Joke Books
- Exploring Emotions
- Self-discovery
- Fantasy
- Independence Themes
- Tongue Twisters and Nonsense
- Books that are just a little Scary (sometimes)
- Friendship Themes
- Extending the Imagination
- Books that Answer Questions about the World
- Sibling/family Stories
- Absurd Situations
- Poetry and Mother Goose Rhymes

Specific Favorites

- *Sing a Song of Popcorn* by Beatrice Schnek Regniers
- *Rotten Ralph's Show and Tell* by Jack Gantos
- *Carl Goes Shopping* by Alexandra Day
- *Corduroy* by Don Freeman
- *King Bidgood's Bathtub* by Audrey Wood
- *Guess What?* by Beau Gardner
- *Goodnight Moon* by Margaret Wish Brown
- *A Hole is To Dig* by Ruth Krauss
- *The Carrot Seed* by Ruth Krauss
- *The Grouchy Lady Bug* by Eric Carl
- *Brown Bear, Brown Bear* by Eric Carl
- *The Napping House* by Charlotte Zolotow
- *Danny and His Thumb* by Kathryn Ernst
- *The Important Book* by Marget Wise Brown
- *Cat in the Hat* by Dr. Suess
- *The Life Sized Animal Counting Book* by Jane Bunting
- *The Amazing Book of Shapes* by Jane Bunting
- *The Polar Express* by Chris Van Allsburg
- *Sheep in Series* by Margot Apple

Story Star

What Do I Learn?

- Emergent Literary Skills
- Listening Comprehension Skills
- Deductive Reasoning

What Do I Learn?

- Chalkboard, Flip Chart, or Overhead Projector
- Story

What Do I Do?

The story star is an easy way to evaluate listening comprehension. Draw the star on the flip chart, or blackboard, or on a transparency sheet for the overhead projector. Ask the children questions like "Where did the story take place? Where was _____ (character's name)? What happened?" This approach will help the children organize their thoughts about the story, as well as review how attentive they were to the story.

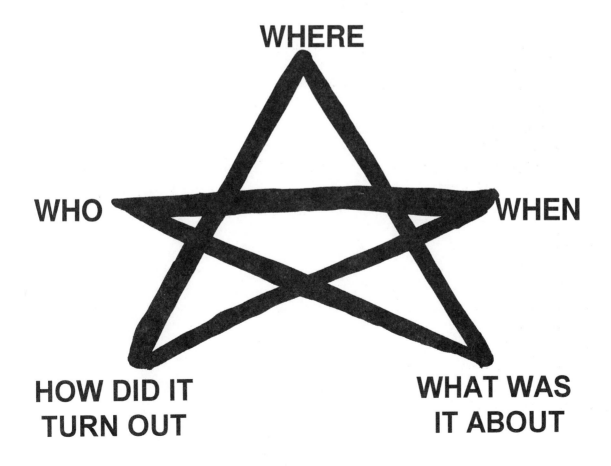

Story Star

WHERE

WHO

WHEN

HOW DID IT
TURN OUT

WHAT WAS
IT ABOUT

SAMPLE STORY STAR
Humpty Dumpty

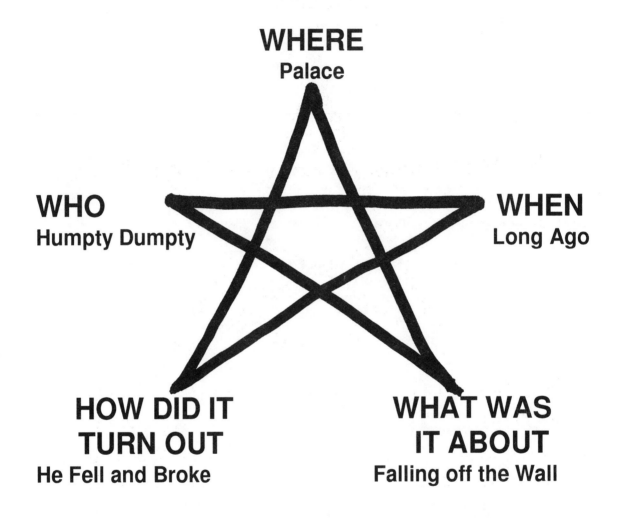

WHERE
Palace

WHO
Humpty Dumpty

WHEN
Long Ago

**HOW DID IT
TURN OUT**
He Fell and Broke

**WHAT WAS
IT ABOUT**
Falling off the Wall

Another Sample Story Star
Goldilocks and the Three Bears

WHERE
The Woods

WHO
Goldi, Mama,
Papa, Baby Bear

WHEN
Yesterday

**HOW DID IT
TURN OUT**
Goldi ran away,
Baby Bear was hungry

**WHAT WAS
IT ABOUT**
Goldi ate their food
and slept in their beds

♥ Felt Boards

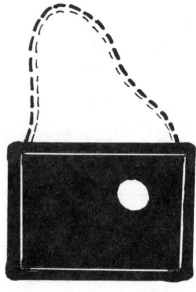

What Do I Learn?
- Emergent Literacy Skills
- Language Skills

What Do I Need?
- Collage Trays
- Felt Squares
- Glue
- Yarn
- Hole Punch
- Yarn

What Do I Do?
Give each child a collage tray. Let the children glue the felt to the board. Punch 2 holes at the top and thread yarn through. Now you have a felt board to wear around your neck.

What Else?
Give the children some felt to tell their own stories. Place several of these felt boards in the reading corner to motivate storytelling. Take the boards home for a family storytelling time.

"Books About Us" Class Book

What Do I Learn?
- Emergent Literacy Skills
- Language Skills

What Do I Need?
- Snapshots
- Tagboard
- Metal Rings
- Hole Punch

What Do I Do?

Ask the children to bring snapshots of themselves engaged in some activities. Try your hand at poetry as you help them create a class book. Glue a picture on each page. Punch holes at the top and add metal rings to create a flip book.
Your book might look like this:

Shrego's sitting in a chair.
Rosa has wind blowing in her hair.

Kristy is playing with her dog.
Marcus likes to take a jog.

Wendy is eating birthday cake.
Eliena sails upon the lake.

What Else?

Can the children help create the rhymes? Write their rhymes as the children dictate.

 **Wordless Text Books**

What Do I Learn?
- Emergent Language Skills
- Literacy Skills

What Do I Need?
- Wordless Text books (*Carl at Day Care, A Day in the Park,* or *Carl's Christmas* by Alexandra Day, *Santa's Long and Difficult Journey* by Fernando Krahn)
- Post- it Notes

What Do I Do?
Select a wordless text book to read to the class. As you look at the pictures, encourage the children to dictate the words. Write their suggestions on post-it notes and place the notes on each page. Now you have created a classroom of young authors!

What Else?
Read the children's works at a parents' meeting.

Copy the text the children provided. Then repeat the activity a few months later. Note the improvement in language skills.

Interactive Language Experience Chart

What Do I Learn?

- Emergent Literacy Skills
- Directionality
- Spatial Concepts
- Listening Skills

What Do I Need?

- Language Chart
- Markers
- Post-it Notes
- A Story

What Do I Do?

Have the children dictate a story; write it in big letters on a chart. After you have read it aloud together, give each child a post-it note. This helps each one to know he/she will be given a turn. Provide the children with opportunities to place their post-it notes on the chart.

SAMPLE STORY ILLUSTRATION

Today we had Olympics at school. We ran and jumped. We had balloon races and Rachel won. Every class made up 2 events. We all won in the end. One boy in Mrs. Lee's class fell and went to the clinic. After the awards, we had lemonade and popsicles. It was fun. We were all hot and tired.

By Mrs. Graham's Authors

Authors' Names (List the children's names or let the children write their own).

QUESTIONS

1. Who can put their post it note on the name of the person who won the race?
2. Who can put their post-it note at the Top of the page? The Bottom?
3. Where does the story End? Start?
4. Who can place their post-it on a number?
5. Can anyone find a letter like one in his/her name?

What Else?

Make a copy of the story to be sent home and "read" to families.

 Washable Mini-Stampers

What Do I Learn?
- Literacy Skills
- Fine Motor Skills
- Creativity

What Do I Need?
- Washable Mini Stampers
- Construction Paper
- Stapler/Staples

What Do I Do?

Make several "books" for your children by folding 4 sheets of paper in half and stapling the edges. Place the books in the Writing Center. Ask the children to stamp a frame around each page. Leave the books in the center for other children to draw or stamp pictures inside the books.

You can make your own mini stampers by cutting small shapes (like hearts, rainbows, circles, triangles, fruits) out of thin sponges.

What Else?

Use the mini stampers to create bookmarks, bookplates, notecards, stationery, or greeting cards to give as presents.

Read *What Do Authors Do?* by Eileen Christelow.

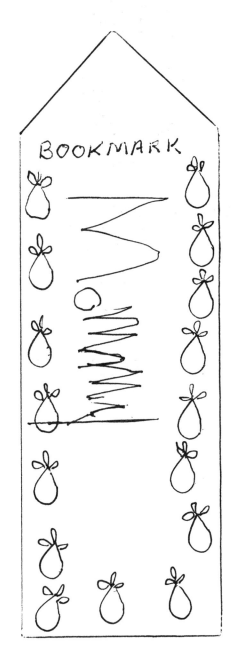

BOOKMARK

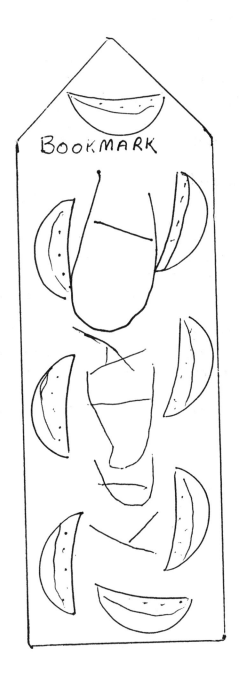

BOOKMARK

♥ Button Bag Book

What Do I Learn?
- Colors
- Language Skills
- Critical Thinking Skills

What Do I Need?
- 2 Felt Rectangles
- Crayons
- 4 Craft Bags
- Colorful Buttons

What Do I Do?
Cut the felt to match the size of the bags. Staple the felt, (one piece for a cover and one for a back), and the 4 bags together to create book pages. Use the text below to write your book, or have the children tell you what the colored buttons are like. When the text is complete, let the children choose buttons to glue on each page. Store some extra buttons inside the bags for the children to match to the pages.

Page 1:
Buttons red, like the brick schoolhouse on the corner.

Page 2:
Buttons blue, like a balloon floating in the azure sky.

Page 3:
Buttons yellow, like butterflies whispering to the wind.

Page 4:
Buttons brown, white, black, and tan like the hands of my friends, clapping and cheering for each other.

What Else?
Let the children take the book home to "read" to their families.
Place the book in your classroom reading center.
Read the story about *Corduroy* by Don Freeman. What happened to his button?

 Author's Suitcase

What Do I Learn?
- Emergent Literacy Skills
- Fine Motor Skills

What Do I Need?
- An Old Suitcase or Briefcase
- Materials for Creating Books/Stories

What Do I Do?
Use an old briefcase or small suitcase for a mobile writing center. Fill it with paper, yarn, metal rings, and other book publishing materials. Let the children take turns taking the suitcase home to create books with their families. Remember that "scribbles" and drawing pictures represent beginning writing communications. Parents should be aware of emergent writing skills too. Make sure that parents supervise; not all materials are suitable for threes on their own (for example, a stapler).

What Else?
Attach this note to your suitcase:
Note to Families
The briefcase may be kept for 3 days. Write a story, color a picture, or do a special project together. Return the briefcase with a sample of your work that can be shared with the class.

Create an authors' bulletin board with the names of the children who have shared this experience at home.

The Message Center

What Do I Learn?
- Emergent Literacy Skills
- Friendship/Socialization Skills

What Do I Need?
- Message Center/Shoe Boxes
- Paper
- Markers, Pencils, Crayons
- Envelopes
- Stamps, Stamp Pads
- Stickers

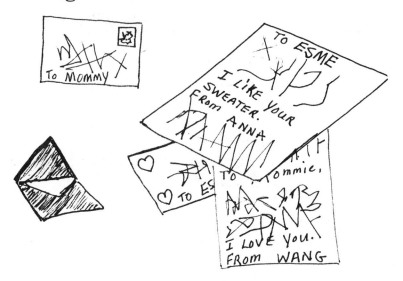

What Do I Do?
There are commercially made mailbox compartments or you can staple several shoe boxes together. Write each child's name, with his or her symbol, on the box. Help the children "write" and deliver messages to each other. You may want to add a translation.

What Else?
At nap time, let the children "read" their mail, with your help.

Beginning Story Telling for Threes:
The Progressive Story

What Do I Learn?
- Concept of a Story
- Emergent Literacy Skills

What Do I Need?
- Laminate a Copy of the Chart Below on Large Chart Paper
- Transparency Markers

What Do I Do?
Tell the children you are going to write a story. Ask them to dictate answers as you fill in the blanks.

The girl's name was_____.
The boy's name was_____.
It happened_____(when).
How was the weather?_____.
Where_____.
The boy was wearing_____.
The girl was wearing_____.
The boy was_____(doing)
The girl was_____(doing)
The boy said,"_____."
The girl said,"_____."
The news on TV said_____.
What happened afterward?_____.

What Else?
Read their answers back to them as you would read a story. Example:

Ritzy and John met yesterday in the Head Start Center - it was a rainy day. John had on his jacket and blue jeans. Ritzy wore her white boots. John was playing in housekeeping and Ritzy was playing in blocks. John said, "Is it rest time yet?" and Ritzy said, "Today is my birthday." When they turned on the news they heard about the bad tornado. Afterward they went on a picnic and lived happily ever after.

As you repeat this activity, children will be able to add more detail. When they say, "a shirt" say, "Tell me more about the shirt." Try for more creative endings than "they lived happily ever after."

When you read the story back, leave parts out for the children to fill in. You'll be surprised at how much they remember.

Potpourri of Literacy

1. Joke Day

Designate one day of the week as JOKE DAY. Anyone can tell a joke and threes love 'Knock Knock' jokes. Jokes are mini-stories and make excellent language builders.

2. See the Sign

Create UNDER CONSTRUCTION signs for your Block Area. This indicates that a structure should not be knocked down and can be completed at another time.

3. Story Aprons

Wear an apron with pockets when you are going to tell a story. This action will also help children get ready to listen when they see you wearing the special story time apron. Hide story props, poems, or rhymes in the pockets. Threes love surprises.

Keep a book in your pocket,
And a poem in your head.
And you'll never be lonely
At night when you're in bed.

4. Name Cards

"I want to be first" and "Whose turn is it ?" can be solved easily. Write each child's name and symbol on a 3x5 note card. Punch a hole in the corner and add a small metal ring.

When the time comes to choose a leader or any other helper, look to see whose name is on the next card. Show the children whose name will come up next so they will always know that their turn will come.

5. Logo Loco

Cut product logos from packages or advertisements. How many can the children identify? (Samples: McDonalds, Crayola, Kellogg's, K-Mart, Toys R Us)

6. Room Poetry

Help the children with their rhyming skills. Ask each child to bring an object from the classroom to your small group time.

Try to write a poem about the object on a language experience chart. You may have to create the first line and have the children complete the rhyme. Remember that threes' rhymes are sometimes nonsense.

Block

A block is hard and made of wood.
I'd build a tower if I_____ .

Doll

I like to comb her curly hair.
But I don't like to have to ____ .

Car

Our cars are red and yellow and blue,
We lost one outside, and now we have___ .

7. Books on the Go

Fill a basket with board books to carry outside. Create a special reading area or time to meet with individual children to share a book. Board books are durable and can be easily wiped clean.

8. Writers on the Go

Take dry marker boards outdoors too. They provide a peaceful transition activity between active times.

9. Perspective Labels

Place Picture/Word labels at different heights around the room. This stimulates eye movements and attention to detail at different levels. "What does that say on the ceiling?"

10. Vocabulary Labels

Be sure to label the toys, art supplies, blocks, and other materials with a word, shape, or picture. Place these labels on the containers or shelves. Commercially made peel and stick labels work well.

Tell Me A Story

What Do I Learn?
- Language Skills
- Emergent Literary Skills

What Do I Need?
- Interfacing (Pellon); approx. 1 foot
- Markers
- Feltboard (cover a cardboard square with a discarded flannel baby blanket)
- Scissors

What Do I Do?
Trace the patterns from the following pages onto the pellon, then cut them out. Read the story *It Looked Like Spilt Milk* by Charles Shaw to the children. One at a time, place the patterns on the feltboard. Ask the children to identify the shape. Encourage the children to verbalize his or her ideas. There is no real right or wrong answer. "Is it spilt milk?"

What Else?
Place the pellon pieces in a cozy corner for the children to retell the story or make up their own stories on a large flannelboard.

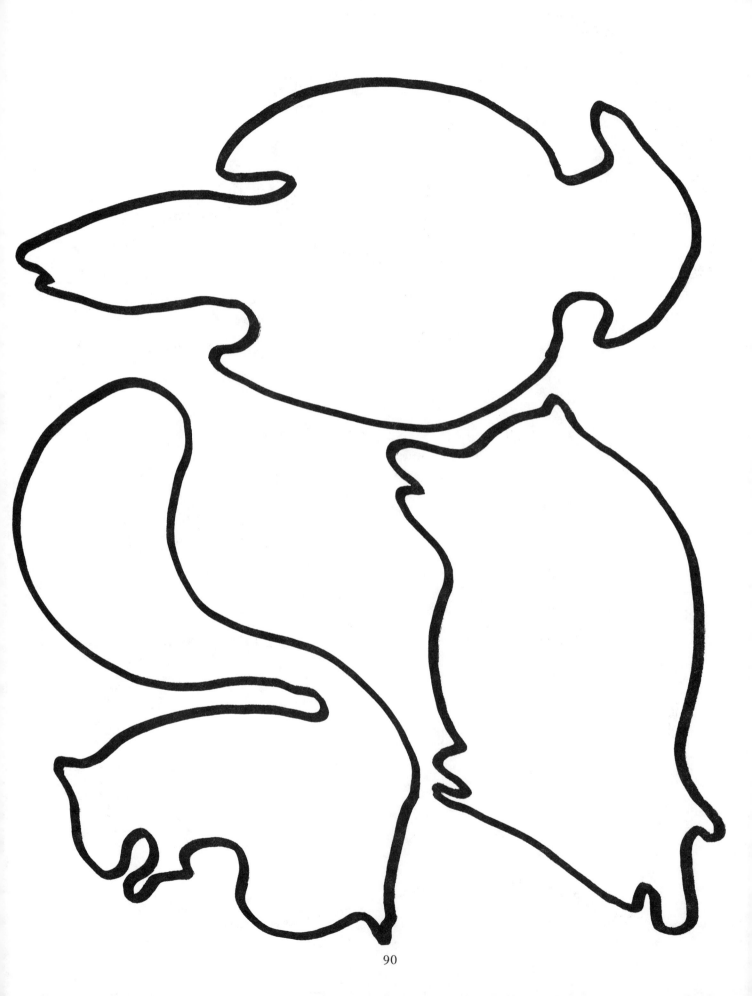

93

Clappertown

Explain to the children that in Clappertown, everyone claps when they hear the words "Doctor" and "Drake". If the words are said together, the people clap twice, but they are very careful not to clap unless they hear one or both words.

Once upon a time a duck got a cold, or what he thought was a cold. "I must go to a doctor (clap once)," said he. "What doctor (clap once) shall it be?"

"Try Doctor Drake (clap twice)." advised a friend. So he went to Doctor Drake (clap twice).

The doctor (clap once) looked over the duck carefully, made him say "aah" while he looked down his throat, thumped his chest, looked stern, and then said "Hmmmmm! You've got the epizoodic."

"The what?" asked the duck.

"The epizoodic, no more, no less." answered Doctor Drake (clap twice).

This made the duck angry. "What a doctor (clap once)!" he stormed. "I'll go to the quack doctor (clap once) and she will fix me as good as new."

"Suit yourself," said Doctor Drake (clap twice).

So the duck went to see the quack doctor (clap once).

"Hmmmmm! Looks like the epizoodic." said the quack doctor (clap once).

"The what?" asked the duck.

"The epizoodic, no more, no less." replied the quack doctor (clap once).

"What will I do?" asked the duck.

"There is only one doctor (clap once) that can cure that." answered the quack doctor (clap once).

"And who is that?" asked the duck.

"Doctor Drake (clap twice). Yes, Doctor Drake (clap twice). You must go to Doctor Drake (clap twice)."

So the duck hurried back to Doctor Drake (clap twice) and Doctor Drake (clap twice) cured him.

Colorful Stories

What Do I Learn?
- Colors
- Listening Comprehension

What Do I Need?
- Story Apron
- Laminated Color Circles

What Do I Do?

Give each child one laminated colored circle: Green, Brown, Red, Black, Blue, Pink, Yellow, Orange, White, Gold, Gray. Tell the children "When you hear your color, stand up. Listen as I tell the story."

Winter Walk

One day Brad and Brittany went for a walk. It was cool outside so Brad wore his red jacket and Brittany wore her yellow wool sweater. They noticed as they walked that the leaves of the trees were turning bright orange, red, and gold. Winter would be here soon and white snow would cover the woods. A furry brown squirrel chattered above their heads as she filled her nest with black nuts for winter. Brad and Brittany noticed that it was getting late and the clear blue sky was turning steel gray. Black crows cawed, signaling the end of the day, and the children knew it was time to get home. As they walked home, they collected a bouquet for Mother of red, yellow, orange, gray, green, white, brown, pink, black, and blue flowers. Mother thanked Brad and Brittany and kissed their pink cheeks.

Daddy's Trick

Mother was going to work. She grabbed her brown pocketbook and headed for the door.

"I'll be home for dinner." she called.

Daddy was thinking "What shall we have for dinner?"

Nancy said "I'm tired of the same old thing!" "Me, too" said little Gary.

"Let's surprise Mom tonight" said Daddy with a twinkle in his eye. He got white milk, yellow butter, yellow corn, and an orange from the refrigerator. From the cabinet above the stove he took out a box of food coloring. The children looked puzzled. What was Daddy up to?

Daddy added a drop of red food coloring to the milk. Presto! Red milk! He cooked the corn in a large pot of water. He carefully added three drops of green food coloring. Into the blender went the butter and the blue food coloring. The orange he left alone. The children laughed when they saw red milk, green corn-on-the-cob, and blue butter.

When Mother came home and saw the strange dinner she did not laugh at first. She turned green! So Dad said "Let's go out to eat." Everyone cheered and headed towards the gray family van.

The Fidgit Family

Give each child the name of one of the characters (one child can be more than one part if there aren't enough children, or two children can be one part if there aren't enough parts). As each name is called in the story, the child rises, turns around, and sits down again. When 'Fidgit Family' is mentioned, everyone gets up and turns around.

Once upon a time there was a family by the name of Fidgit. There was Pa Fidgit, Ma Fidgit, Maggie Fidgit, Johnny Fidgit, Bridgit Fidgit, Sammie Fidgit, the Twins, and Baby Fidgit.

One day Ma Fidgit said to Pa Fidgit, "Suppose we hitch Old Moll and Old Doll to the wagon and spend the night at Grandma and Grandpa Fidgit's?" Pa said "All right." He got Maggie and Johnnie, Sammie and Bridgit, the Twins and Baby Fidgit all ready while Ma hitched Old Doll and Old Moll up to the wagon, so all could go to Grandpa and Grandma Fidgit's house.

Ma Fidgit drove the wagon around to the front of the house, and Johnnie and Maggie and Bridgit and Sammie all ran out to the wagon and got in. Then Pa Fidgit came out with the Baby, got into the wagon, and handed the Baby to Ma Fidgit. Then Pa Fidgit started up Old Doll and Old Moll and the wagon and away they went to the house of Grandma and Grandpa Fidgit. But in the rush Pa Fidgit forgot the Twins and Ma Fidgit forgot her pocketbook, so Pa Fidgit stopped Old Doll and Old Moll and the wagon and sent Sammie and Johnnie back to where the Twins were sitting by the side of the house. Sammie and Johnnie made the Twins run and get in the wagon, and then got Ma Fidgit's pocketbook. Pa Fidgit started up Old Moll and Old Doll and the wagon again and they were on the way to Grandpa and Grandma Fidgit's house.

When they arrived, Bridgit and Sammie and Maggie and the Twins all jumped out of the wagon and Ma Fidgit, with Baby on one arm and her pocketbook on the other, got out. There were Grandma and Grandpa Fidgit running from the house to greet them. Grandpa Fidgit helped Pa Fidgit unhitch Old Doll and Old Moll from the wagon. Then Grandma Fidgit went with Ma Fidgit up the walk to the house carrying Baby Fidgit and the pocketbook, and there were Maggie, Sammie, Bridgit, and Johnnie running up to the house with the Twins bringing up the rear. When Grandpa and Pa Fidgit came from unhitching Old Doll and Old Moll from the wagon, Grandma Fidgit had dinner ready and the whole Fidgit family had a wonderful time at the dinner at Grandma and Grandpa Fidgit's house.

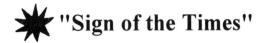 **"Sign of the Times"**

What Do I Learn?
- Cultural Awareness
- Emergent Literacy Skills

What Do I Need?
- Copy of the Sign Language Alphabet (see following page)

What Do I Do?
     Teach the children some simple signs (like the sign for I love you). You may want to create some sign language alphabet or number flash cards. Talk about what it means to be "hearing impaired." Put earphones on some of the children and speak to them. How did they feel when they couldn't hear? There are also commercially made dolls with hearing aides and other special needs. You'll want to include them in your classroom materials. (People of Every Stripe Company, California)

What Else?
     Read *Friends in the Park, Friends at School* by Rochelle Bunnett.

     Obtain copies of *Mother Goose in Sign, A Word in Hand, Animal Signs,* and *The Finger Alphabet,* all by Linda Bove.

I LOVE YOU

Catch The Creative Spirit:
What Can I Do?

Science, Math, and Music
Cooking, Dance, and Art,
Threes catch the creative spirit,
With activities from the heart!

Scissors, colored paper, bottles filled with glue,
I love to make my pictures, there's so much here to do.
I paint or cut or color, until it's clean-up time,
Then give my art to Mommy,
Who loves it cause it's mine.

*Children need to associate learning with creativity. Science and math don't have to hard, or difficult to understand. Each can be just as creative as art or music. The process the teacher uses to introduce concepts and activities should be **creative** and hands on. For this reason, science and math are considered as a creative part of threes' curriculum.*

Tips For Threes' Art Experiences

- Keep activities simple.
- Think "process, not product".
- Three year olds are at a variety of stages in art. Be accepting.
- Share what you know about each child's art with parents.   Keep samples of a child's art in a portfolio: it is helpful at conference time.
- **Clean-up** is part of the process.
- Three year olds like to take their projects home, but it's a good time to start projects that cannot be completed in one session.

DALE M.

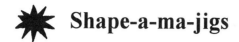 **Shape-a-ma-jigs**

What Do I Learn?
- Fine Motor Skills
- Shape/Color Recognition

What Do I Need?
- Easy Grip Scissors
- Shape Stencils or Pre-cut Shapes
- Crayons/Write Start Pencils
- Yarn
- Hole Punch

What Do I Do?
Cut out 2 squares or 2 circles or 2 triangles for each child, using the following patterns. Draw a dotted line half way up on each shape. Help the child cut on the dotted line of each shape. Fit the 2 circles, 2 squares, or 2 triangles together. Punch a hole in the top of each new shape and add yarn. Hang your Shape-a-ma-jigs from the ceiling or doorway.

What Else?
Mix the shapes to create new shapes: Tri-circles, Tri-squares, or Cir-angles.

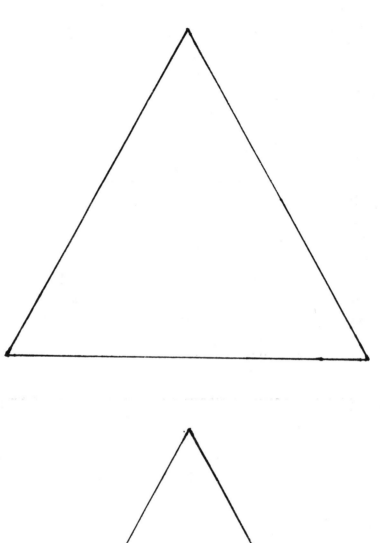

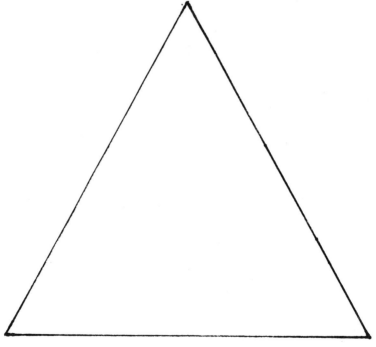

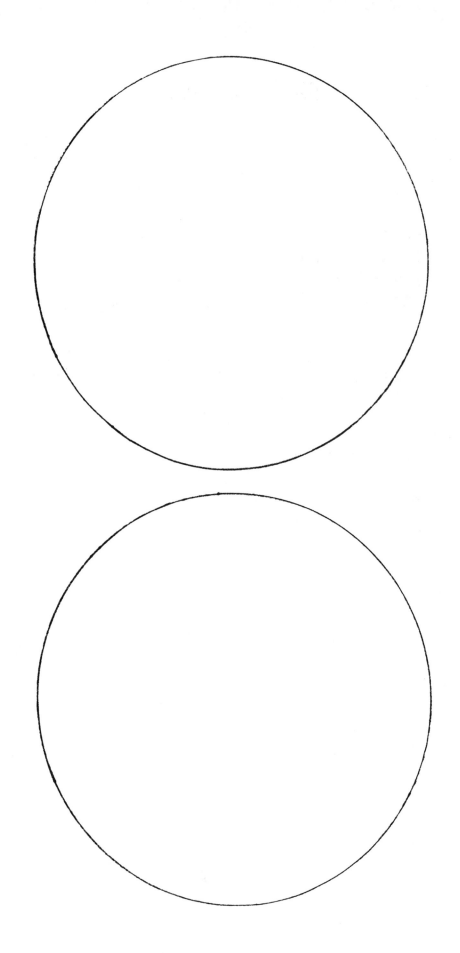

 **Sticker-Pix**

What Do I Learn?
- Fine Motor Skills
- Classification Skills
- Language Skills

What Do I Need?
- Crayons/Markers/Write Start Pencils
- White Construction Paper
- Stickers

What Do I Do?
Let each child select 5 stickers that belong to the same category (All animals/fruits). Place the stickers randomly on the paper. Draw a large DOT next to each sticker. Help the child draw lines connecting all the stickers.

What Else?
Use rubber stamps and washable ink pad to create the same experience.

 **Name Puzzles**

What Do I Learn?
- Fine Motor Skills
- Name/Letter Recognition

What Do I Need?
- Tagboard
- Zig-zag Scissors or Pinking Shears
- Markers

What Do I Do?
Have an adult write your name in BIG sized letters. Remember to begin with an uppercase letter, followed by lowercase letters. They'll cut it apart for you into puzzle pieces, with special scissors. Mix up the letters. Can you put your name puzzle together?

What Else?
Can you make name puzzles for other people in your family?

 # Rings and Circles Are Round and Round

What Do I Learn?
- Shape/Color Recognition
- Fine Motor Skills

What Do I Need?

- Round Things - Spools, Corks, Lids, and Caps
- Tempera Paint or Washable Stamp Pads
- Fine-tip Markers or Crayons
- Paper

What Do I Do?
Use the round objects to print or stamp circles on the paper. Let the "circles dry overnight". Use the fine-tipped markers to create pictures from the circles (flowers, insects, people).

What Else?
Play a circle game like Ring Around the Rosey, Farmer in the Dell, or Duck, Duck, Goose.

Paper Towel Crunch

What Do I Learn?
- Language Skills
- Fine Motor Skills
- Discovery Skills

What Do I Need?
- Food Coloring
- Tubs for water (This center can be at the water table.)
- Paper Towels

What Do I Do?
Scribble or draw a picture on the paper towel. Press hard. Crunch your picture up. Dip it in the colored water. Open your towel and lay it flat to dry. Tell about the colors you see.

What Else?
Read *Mouse Paint* by Ellen Stoll Wash.

Rainbow Colors

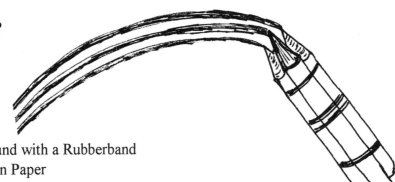

What Do I Learn?
- Color Recognition
- Creativity
- Fine Motor Skills

What Do I Need?
- Three crayons Bound with a Rubberband
- 18x12 Construction Paper

What Do I Do?
Help the children grip the crayons. Tape the paper down so that it won't move while they color. Create! How do those colors look?

What Else?
Read *Land of Colors* from the Poke and Look Series.

What Color Is This?

What Do I Learn?
- Color Recognition
- Language Skills
- Prediction

What Do I Need?
- Color Paddles
- Play-Doh

What Do I Do?
   Add the color paddles to your play-dough supplies. Let the children experiment with creating different colors. "If I make a red snake, what color will it be when I look through the red paddle?"

What Else?
   Let the children make their own color paddles with cellophane and tagboard.

Frame It!

What Do I Learn?
- Temporal Concepts: Day and Night

What Do I Need?
- Two 4x6 Pre-Cut Mat Frames
- Cellophane
- Construction Paper cut in 4x6 Rectangles
- Blue and Yellow Cellophane cut in 4x6 Rectangles
- Crayons
- Glue

What Do I Do?
Glue one frame to the blue cellophane and one frame to the yellow cellophane. You now have a Day Board and a Night Board, respectively.

Draw a picture on your construction paper of something you do at night. Turn the paper over and draw a picture of something you do during the day. Use your Day/Night Boards to cover your pictures. How do the pictures change?

What Else?
Create a Day and Night Time Center. Cut out pictures from magazines. Glue them to tag board and laminate. Place the pictures and some Day/Night Boards in the center. Encourage the children to look at the pictures and decide what time the pictures take place.

For additional Day/Night activities, read *Sunny Days and Starry Nights* by Nancy Castalgo.

Graphs on the Ground

What Do I Learn?
- Science/Math Skills
- Counting

What Do I Need?
- Mural Paper/laminated
- Transparency Markers
- Permanent Markers
- Optional: Bean Bags/ Plastic Vehicles/ Counters/ Stickers/ Post-it Notes

What Do I Do?
Create a grid on the mural paper and laminate it. Use it for graphing any theme related activity. Use the markers to label the squares or add picture symbols the children will recognize.

What Else?
Use the following suggestions for your graph on the ground.

How Do We Get Here Graph
- Ask "How many children ride the bus to school? Walk? Carpool?"
- Have the children place a cut out bus, car, or next to their names.

Family Graph

- List the names of the children down one side of the grid.
- List family members, and pets, of course, across the top.

Favorite Foods Graph

- Cut out vegetable shapes and place them across the top.
- Ask the children which ones they like.

Shoe Graph

- Cut out the patterns; Tie Shoes/ Velcro Shoes /Buckle Shoes/ Slippers/ Boots and put them on post-it notes at the top of the page.
- Have the children write their name or draw/glue their symbols under the type of shoe they wear.

 # ♥ Write About It

What Do I Learn?
- Math Skills
- Science Skills
- Emergent Literacy Skills
- Language Skills

What Do I Need?
- Language Experience Chart Paper
- Markers

What Do I Do?
Before each graphing experience, ask the children what they think they will find out. Record their predictions. Will there be more children who walk to school or take the bus?

After each graphing experience, bring the children together to talk about it. How did we start? What did we do? What did we find out?

What Else?
Copy the graphing experience story and send it home for the children to "read" to their families. What can they graph at home? Try: Showers and Baths, Likes and Dislikes.

SNAP

What Do I Learn?
- Spatial Relationships
- Language Skills
- Gross Motor Skills
- Following Directions

What Do I Need?
- Shape Set

What Do I Do?
Put the _____ over your head.
Put the _____ behind you.
Stand on the _____.
Skip around the _____.
Hop over the _____.
Give your shape to a friend.
Line the shapes up and walk between them.

What Else?
Use bean bags or koosh balls to extend the activity:
Say "Throw your beanbag over the square. Hide your beanbag under the triangle."

 **Fun Foam Shape Boards**

What Do I Learn?
- Shape Recognition
- Language Skills
- Social Skills
- Parent Involvement

What Do I Need?
- Fun Foam Shapes
- Glue
- Collage Tray

What Do I Do?
Glue several shapes to the collage tray: use the shape patterns on the following pages and cut shapes from foam or sponges.

Cover the child's eyes and ask him to touch a shape. "Can you describe it? Tell a friend what the shape feels like. What shape is it? Can you draw it?"

What Else?
Make a board to take home. Let the children teach their parents how to play the game. Earn a hug each time you guess the right shape!

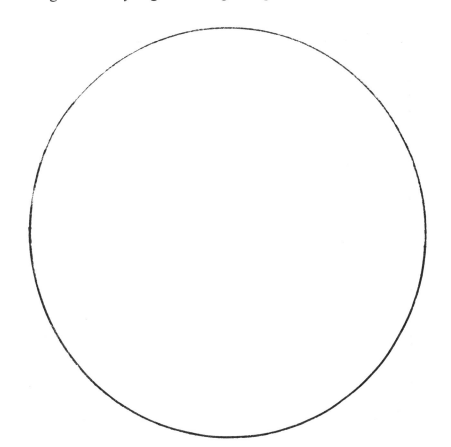

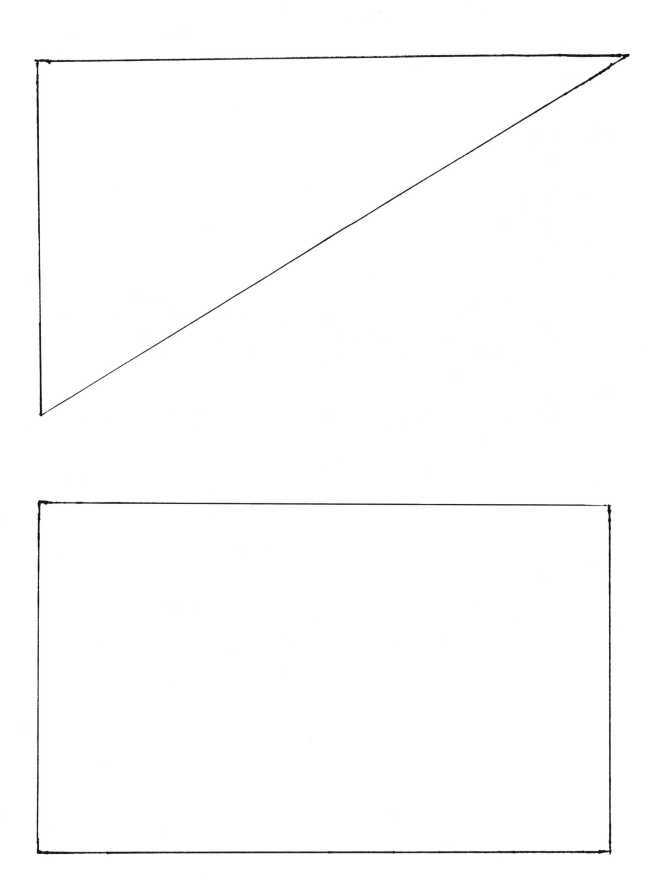

Have A Ball

What Do I Learn?
- Tactile Discrimination
- Memory

What Do I Need?
- 2 Koosh Balls
- 2 Beanbags
- 2 Foam Balls
- 2 Tennis Balls
- 2 Ping Pong Balls

What Do I Do?
Place one of each of the above balls in a large bag or box. Line the other set of balls on a table. Let the children touch each of the balls. Now have each child reach in the bag and touch one of the balls. Describe the ball. Is it hard? Soft? What game can you play with it? Can the child correctly match it to one of the balls on the table?

What Else?
Roll the balls on an incline. Which goes faster? Use a stop watch to find out.

Take a Step Number Hunt

What Do I Learn?

- Number Concepts

What Do I Need?

- Number Steps

What Do I Do?

Place the numbers around your outdoor play area. Ask the children to find things in the environment to equal the number on the step. Example: #6, six leaves.

What Else?

Create a language experience story about the children's finds.
"On Monday, we found 1 rock. On Tuesday, we found 2 feathers."

Literacy Count

What Do I Learn?

- Counting Skills
- One to One Correspondence
- Literacy and Language Skills

What Do I Need?

- Abacus
- *A Very Hungry Caterpillar* by Eric Carl

What Do I Do?

Read the story to the children. Each time the caterpillar samples a new morsel, have a child move one bead over. How many things did he eat in all?

What Else?

Move yellow beads for sweets, green beads for vegetables, red beads for meats. Did the caterpillar eat more nutritious foods or unhealthy foods?

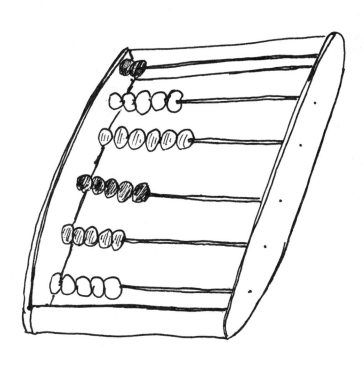

Let's Cook!
What's Cookin'?

Stirring, mixing, rolling,
Recipes from our book,
Spilling, laughing, tasting,
Threes sure love to cook!

WASH HANDS

SOAP

Veggie Scrub

What Do I Learn?
- Fine Motor Skills
- Language Skills
- Health/nutrition Concepts

What Do I Need?
- Assorted Vegetables (Carrots, Potatoes, Celery Sticks)
- Small Brushes
- Plastic Tubs of Water
- Paper Towels

What Do I Do?
WASH HANDS. Place veggies in tub. Scrub with small brushes.
Have your teacher help you slice the veggies into bite-sized pieces. Dip in Healthy Yogurt
Delight!

Healthy Yogurt Delight

What Do I Need?
- 1 pint Plain Lowfat Yogurt
- 1/4 Cup Lowfat Mayo
- Pinch of Lemon Pepper Seasoning

What Do I Do?
Mix! Dip!

What Else?
Read *Vegetables* by Douglas Florian
Play "Find the Veggies". Hide plastic vegetables around the room or outside. Help
the children name each vegetable.

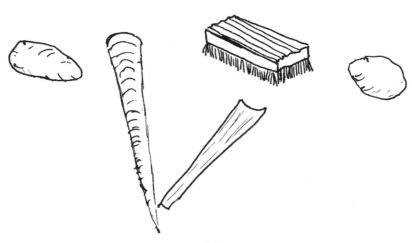

ABC Fruit Bars

What Do I Learn?
- Language Skills
- Health/nutrition Concepts
- Fine Motor Skills

What Do I Need?
- Plastic Alphabet Molds
- Melt 5 TBS. Raspberry AllFruit Jam
- 2/3 Cup Lowfat Strawberry Yogurt
- Canned Fruit (optional)
- Cooking Tools

What Do I Do?
WASH HANDS. Mix yogurt and melted raspberry All Fruit. Pour into molds. Put in freezer while you play outside. Pop out of mold or eat with sample ice cream spoons.

What Else?
Song "Juanito Ate A Little J"
Tune:" Mary Had A Little Lamb"

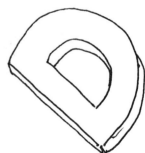

Juanito ate a little J
Little J, little J
Juanito ate a little J
(Clap)J!J!J!J!J!
     OR
Brittany ate a little B
Little B, little B
Brittany ate a little B
It made her big and brave!

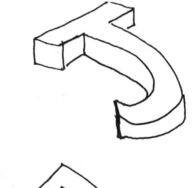

Tic Tac Toast

What Do I Learn?
- Symbol Recognition
- Spatial Concepts
- Language Skills

What Do I Need?
- Bread
- Can of Easy Cheese Spread, Black Olive Slices, Low Fat Cheese Slices
- Cooking Tools

What Do I Do?
Lay a slice of cheese on top of a slice of bread. Heat until cheese is melted. Draw Tic Tac Toe lines on the bread with the Easy Cheese Spread. Make X's with Easy Cheese and use black olives for O's.

What Else?
Play Tic Tac Toe outside.

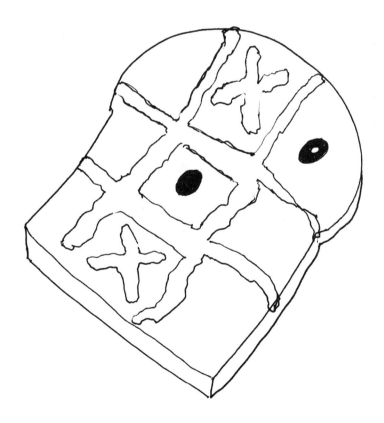

Coolie Smoothie

What Do I Learn?
- Nutrition Concepts
- Language Skills
- Fine Motor Skills
- Life Skills

What Do I Need?
- Oranges, Bananas
- Shredded Coconut
- Fruit Juices
- Straws, Cups, and Plastic Knives
- Blender

What Do I Do?
Peel banana and chop into blender. Cut oranges in half. Squeeze oranges and add juice. Add 1/2 cup of any juice. Blend and pour into cup. Top with shredded coconut.

What Else?
Serve after exercise. Makes a nutritious pick-me-up.

On Beyond
"What Color Is This?"
What Can I Think?

Thinking About Tomorrow
For all that we are doing for the children of today,
We prepare them for the future by the things we do & say.
There is a bright tomorrow, and we teachers are the link.
Dreams can come true for children,
If we give them time to THINK!

Critical Thinking Skills for Threes

Most of us, when we were in school, were not taught to think critically or to question. We conformed to the norm, circled the right answer, or filled in the blank to a question that had one right answer. If we teach children the same way we were taught, we do them a disservice. Today's world wants thinkers, questioners, and risk takers. Our childrens' futures lie in their abilities to come up with many possible answers, to prioritize, and to be good problem solvers. Threes are not too young to become the critical thinkers of tomorrow when teachers ask the right questions today.

Why teach critical thinking?

- Asking the right questions challenges thinking to a higher level.
- There is often more than one right answer.
- Social and cooperative skills are enhanced.
- Emphasizes producing life long thinkers.
- Encourages long term projects.
- Helps develop better writing skills.
- Develops an awareness of thinking.

How Can We Teach Thinking Skills?

If questioning is the key, then planning is the door. Learn the questioning strategies in this chapter and plan for them.

Teachers need time to practice their critical thinking skills. Use staff and parent meetings, newsletters, and your daily routine to plan for critical thinking.

Teaching children to name colors is a good place to start, and usually the place where good thinking ends too! We begin with, "Show me the red block. Where is the blue car?" Then as the receptive vocabulary develops, we move to, "What color is this?" And then we stop.

- Find as many red things as you can.
- Do you like red?
- List all the shades of red.
- What is NOT red?
- If red could talk....
- _____-is red.
- _____are red.

For a different color song, learn the Color Rap.

Note: The first and third line can, but do not have to rhyme. Encourage children to use the senses clues to think of creative color answers. The teacher says each line and the children repeat each line and then create their own last lines.

Color Rap

I know a color and it is GREEN.
Prettiest color you've ever seen.
Green is like_____

I know a color and it is BLUE.
If you see it, you'll like it too.
Blue feels like_____

I know a color and it is RED.
Makes you leap right out of bed.
Red looks like_____

I know a color and it is YELLOW.
Can be loud or can be mellow.
Yellow sounds like_____

I know a color and it is PINK.
If you know it, give a wink.
Pink tastes like_____

I know a color and it is BLACK.
If you know it, pat your back.
Black feels like_____

I know a color and it is BROWN.
Makes you jump both up and down.
If brown could talk, it would say_____

I know a color and it is WHITE.
Wear it when you walk at night.
White smells like_____

Critical Thinking Questioning Strategies

Cut out the following cards and laminate them, punch a hole in the corner, and add a metal ring. You can also take the list of questions which follows and write your own cards. Then you will have an extensive card file to keep with you so that you can ask higher level questions as you interact with your children.

Would you rather?

How is it like?

What would they say?

The answer is......

Paradox

What's the difference?

Ask me a question.

Is it possible?

Reflecting

List the ways...

Compare/Contrast

What does it weigh?

____is bad, but ____is worse.

Critical Thinking Card File

Cut out each strategy, or rewrite onto index cards. Keep them handy for reminding yourself of the many different ways of expanding the way you ask questions.

Would you rather?

Live in a space ship or a submarine?

How is it like?

How is a cave like a motel?

What would...

Groceries say to each other?

The answer is......

The answer is mud, what is the question?

Paradox

What sound does fog make?

What's the difference?

What's the difference between a house and a home?

Ask me a question.

Ask me a question about my teddy bear.

Is it possible?

Is it possible for cave men to make phone calls?

List

List the ways to get a hippo out of the bath

Reflecting

Why are jumbo shrimp small?

What does it weigh?

Which weighs more, a good day or bad?

_____ is bad, but _____ is worse.

Losing is bad, not getting to play is worse.

Compare/Contrast

How are a knock and a rock alike?

Critical Thinking Activities for Threes

Picture File:
Collect interesting pictures, photographs, and greeting cards. Place a peel-off label on the reverse side to write your question. Use the questioning strategies already listed.

- How is sand like snow?

Puzzle Quests
When a child is working a puzzle with large pieces, like the knobbed puzzles, ask...

- What would the apple say to the grapes?

Boxes
Save interesting boxes to hide pennies, buttons, keys, and brushes. Write your questions on note cards.

- How is a button like a penny?
- Is it possible for a brush to meet teeth?

- If a key could talk, what would it say?
- What would a key say to a door?

Color Song Flip Chart

- Color the following pictures with your crayons or markers.
- Laminate the pages.
- Punch holes at the top and add metal rings.
- Flip the pages as the children sing the color song to this tune:

GG/ ECC/ DCBA/ GGG/ GGFE/ DBGG/ GGAB/ C
Encourage the children to create their own verses.

- You can also make copies of these pages and have the children color their own pictures while singing the song!

- **I like green. It's the best for me.**

- **It's the color of the grass, and the color of the sea.**

- **I like red, the color makes me merry.**

- **It's the color of an apple and the color of a cherry.**

- **I like yellow, it's a color just for fun,**

- **It's the color of bananas and the color of the sun.**

- **I like blue, let me tell you why,**

- **It's the color of my crayon and the color of the sky.**

- **I like orange. It's the best of all.**

- **It's the color of my pumpkin, and pretty leaves in the fall.**

- I like brown. It's the best, you see.

- It's the color of tea, and the color of a chocolate chip cookie.

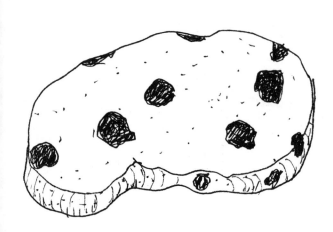

- **I like black. The color is just dandy.**

- **It's the color of thunder, and the color of licorice candy.**

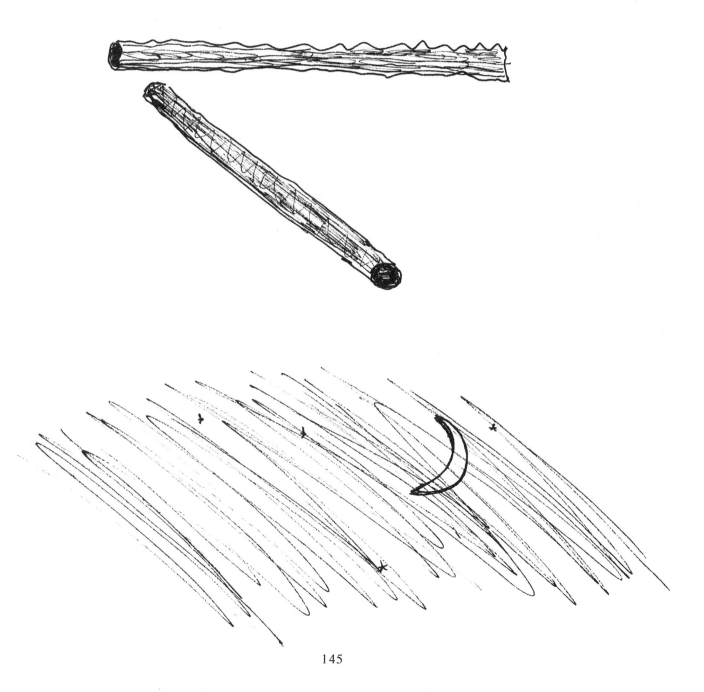

THREES OUTDOORS
Watch Me! Watch Me!

Threes Outdoors...
Run and jump and swing and hide,
Threes just love to play outside.
Paint or read or sit and then,
Rest awhile and back again.

 SUN SMART THREES

What Do I Learn?
- Sun Safety Awareness
- Color Recognition
- Name Recognition

What Do I Need?
- Foam Sheets or Tag Board
- Visor Patterns
- Stickers
- Markers

What Do I Do?
Teacher can cut visors for each child from the following. Add their names.
Let the children decorate their visors with markers or stickers and wear them outside.

What Else?
Talk about sun safety. Children should wear a sunscreen and will enjoy having sunglasses at school for outside play. It's never too early to be SUN SMART.

Talk to parents about the importance of sun safety for their children; copy and distribute the following Sun Smart Checklist to parents.

BEING HEALTHY MEANS BEING SUN SMART

* Wear a hat or visor to protect from the sun.

* Wear sunglasses.

* Use sunscreen, even on cloudy days.

* You need protection from the sun even in winter.

* Avoid tanning.

VISOR

SUN SCREEN LOTION

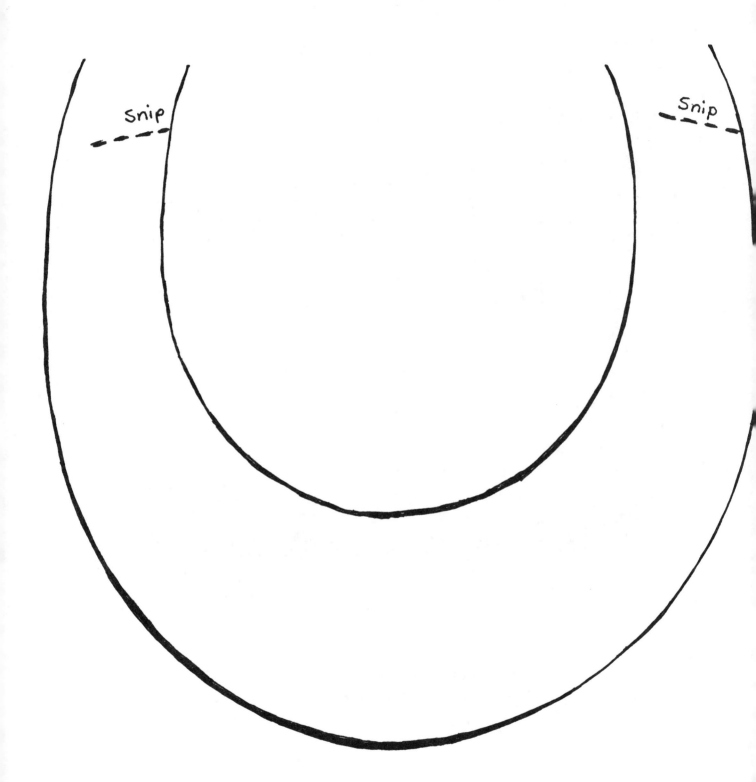

Snip

Snip

❤ Fun At the Fence

What Do I Learn?
- Patterns
- Fine Motor Skills

What Do I Need?
- Wide Ribbon or Fabric
- A Chain Link Fence

What Do I Do?
Give each child a 12" piece of ribbon or fabric. To create patterns, try 2 or three different colors. Show the children how to "weave" the fabric through the holes in the fence. Talk about weaving under and over.

For patterns, weave RED, BLUE, RED **OR:** RED, RED, BLUE, RED, RED, BLUE.

What Else?
Bring different baskets to school. Talk about woven patterns. Look for other patterns outside.

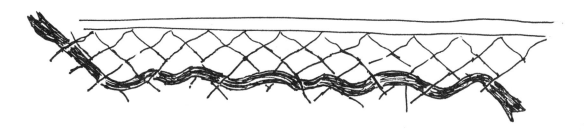

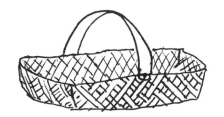

 **At The Fence Again**

What Do I Learn?
- Fine Motor Skills
- Creativity

What Do I Need?
- Sheet of Tissue Paper
- A Chain Link Fence

What Do I Do?
Crush the tissue paper into balls. Leave a little point to stick it into the holes in the fence. Create a design or a collage of colors.

What Else?
Take pictures of the fence: Before/During/After. Talk about the sequence of activities. The after is the clean-up and returning the fence to its original look. Can the paper be used again in an art project?

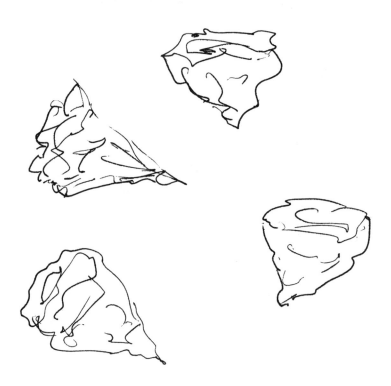

And Again

What Do I Learn?
- Fine Motor Skills
- Life Skills

What Do I Need?
- Spring Hinge Clothespins
- Tub of Water
- Fabric or Doll Clothes

What Do I Do?
Have a MONDAY WASH DAY. Clean fabric scraps or doll clothes and hang them on the fence to dry. Spring hinged clothes pins strengthen the small muscles threes will need later to grip pencils or pens.

What Else?
Sing: "This is the way we wash our clothes"
Tune: "Here We Go 'Round the Mulberry Bush".
Read: *The Day Jimmy's Boa Ate The Wash* by Trinkle Noble

 **No Mess Paint Day**

What Do I Learn?
- Fine Motor Skills
- Gross Motor Skills
- Spatial Relationships

What Do I Need?
- Large, Real Paint Brushes
- Tub of Water

What Do I Do?
Give the children 4" paint brushes and a tub of water. Let them paint the sidewalk or the school. Draw chalk shapes for them and let them paint inside/outside the shape.

What Else?
Give the children a variety of small brushes and compare the different strokes. Which brush makes the biggest lines?

Just before the class comes out, paint several different lines on the sidewalk. Can they guess which brush made which line?

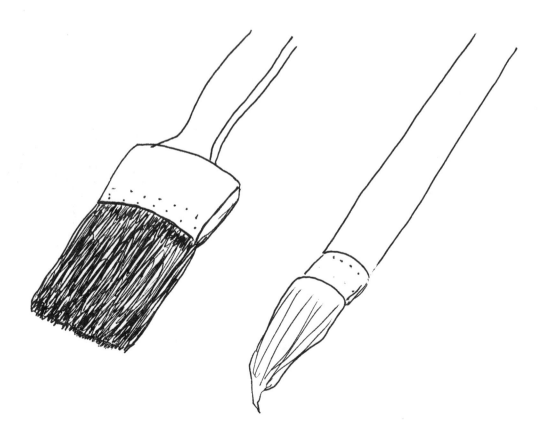

Easels Out

What Do I Learn?
- Spatial Relationships
- Creativity
- Environmental Relationships

What Do I Need?
- Easels in a Shady Spot
- A Mobile Cart with Containers/pans of Paint from which the 3's can select
- Easel Paper

What Do I Do?
"What are you going to use to paint with today? We have no paint brushes."
Encourage the children to find things from nature to use as painting tools. "What kind of line does a twig make? A rock? A leaf?"

What Else?
Move the easel to a sunny place. How do the children's pictures reflect the change in light?

What's Ticking?

What Do I Learn?
- Temporal Concepts
- Listening Skills

What Do I Need?
- Large Sand Box
- Minute Timer in a Plastic Bag

What Do I Do?
Hide the timer in the sand (make sure the plastic bag is sealed tightly- sand can ruin a timer). Tell the children to listen very carefully. "What do you think the sound could be?" Can they find the timer before the bell rings?

What Else?
Make a Time Graph. Let the children work in partners to find the timer. Chart how long each partnership took to find the timer.

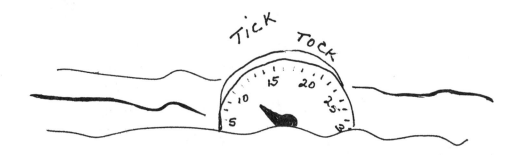

Transitions
How Do I Get From Here to There?

Listen for the signal,
Listen for the song.
There's tricks to making changes
To move the day along

A rhyme, a fingerplay, or a simple song can help children move from activity to activity with ease. Discipline can be done the same way. Here are some simple transitional strategies that you can start using right away.

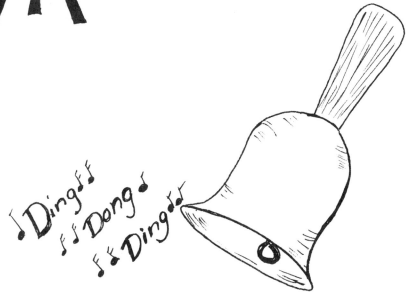

Making Changes and Rearranges:
Transition Tips

1. Signal
Use musical instruments to signal the changing of activities. A bell, triangle, tambourine, or playing the first 4 or 8 notes of Beethoven's 5th Symphony can let children know that work time will soon be over.

2. Whisper Train
Whisper "It's clean up time" to one child. She/he must pass the information on by whispering to another child.

3. Circle Time Songs (Tune: Ten Little Astronauts)
Help children get ready to listen by singing:
"I like the way that Andrea's ready, I like the way that Ben is ready.
I like the way that Jerica's ready, ready to hear a story."

4. Clean-Up Song
"It's clean-up time, It's clean-up time.
Let's put our toys away.
It's clean-up time, It's clean-up time, What did you clean today?"

5. Hats On!
Create a transition hat. Either you can wear the hat, or you can place it on a child. When the other children see the hat, they know it's time for clean-up, rest, or time to come inside.

6. Schedules
Post your daily routine where children can view it. Use symbols the children can recognize to represent elements of the day. Children can place post-it notes next to the activities they have completed.

7. Fingerplays on the Move

Copy some of the fingerplays from *Fingerplays and Rhymes: For Always and Sometimes* (Terry Graham, Humanics Publishing) onto 4x6 index cards. Laminate the cards, punch a hole at the top, and add a metal ring. Then you will always have transitional rhymes at your fingertips.

8. Husha Bunny

Select a stuffed animal that represents time to HUSH! Bring Husha Bunny out when its time to listen to a story or rest quietly. When the children are ready, they can pet the bunny (or horse, pig, mouse, etc.)

9. Who is Ready?

Cut out the bottom of a coffee can or plastic basket. Cover the can with fabric or contact paper. Using a hand puppet (a bunny with long ears is the best), put your arm through one open side and let the bunny appear through the other. Tell the children the puppet will come out when everyone is quiet and still. If the puppet sees anyone wiggling or hears any noise, it goes back into the can.

10. Music Box

Use a music box to help children know how much play time they have left or to indicate other transitions. When the music stops, rest time will begin.

New Rhymes for Transition Times

Nap Time

Wiggle your nose, fingers tap
Now its time to take a nap.

Line Up

First or last, who can be
In line and waiting quietly?

Planning

Who would like to make a plan?
Like artwork, I know you can!
We think, and do, and then we say,
Everything we learned today.

Going Home

If your name begins with B,
Go and get your coat for me.

If you're tall or wearing red,
Get your coat and nod your head.

If you're wearing shoes that tie,
Get your coat and pretend to fly.

If your name rhymes with blue,
You can get your coat on too!

If you have a cat or dog,
Get your coat and leap like a frog.

If you're left, don't make a fuss,
Hurry now and catch the bus.

Transitional Tunes

Select a simple tune you know well and that the children will recognize too:

- Twinkle, Twinkle Little Star
- Mary Had A Little Lamb
- Are You Sleeping?
- Way Down Yonder

1. Ask yourself, "What do I want the children to do?"
2. Choose a song.
3. Create rhymes that go with the song's rhythm.
4. Sing to the children.

Examples:
Tune: Twinkle Twinkle Little Star

Line up. Line up. Straight and tall.
Quietly walking down the hall.
Careful not to talk at all.
Make this sign_____ to one and all.

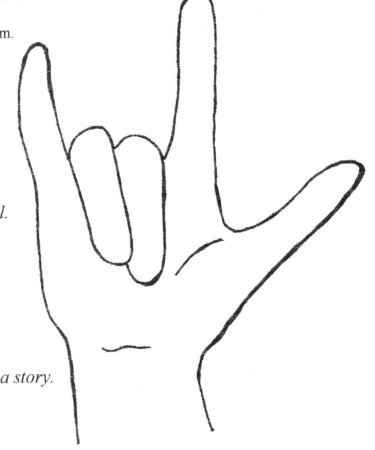

Tune: Are you Sleeping?

Are you ready? Are you ready?
Now show me.
Now show me.
You want to hear a story. Want to hear a story.
Sitting quietly. Sitting quietly.

Now make up a transitional tune of your own.

Tune: Merrily We Roll Along

Now it's time to end this book,
End this book,
End this book.
Now it's time to end this book,
What did you learn today?

NEW PRODUCTS

Teaching Terrific Threes and Other Toddlers

Terry Lynne Graham, M.A.
PAGES: 128 / ISBN: 0-89334-260-2
PRICE: $17.95 / AGES: 3's AND 4's

This long-anticipated sequel to the bestseller *Teaching Terrific Twos* is the ultimate in resource guides for three year olds. Filled with fun and educational activities specifically designed to meet and challenge the abilities and interests of three year olds, *Threes* is a must for anyone involved in caring for this special age group. Activities concentrate on social growth, listening skills, self-image, language skills, fine and gross motor development, and awareness of such concepts as science, math, music, and nutrition. Includes a section about room arrangement, scheduling, discipline, assessment, parent involvement, materials, and basic and individual goals.

Author TERRY GRAHAM is one of the most respected authorities on toddlers' education; her insights are a wonderful addition to any child care library.

Bottle Cap Activities: Recycled Crafts for All Ages

Kathy Cisneros
PAGES: 112 / ISBN: 0-89334-279-3
PRICE: $12.95 / AGES: 7 AND UP

From simple to sophisticated crafts, these innovatively creative projects are made of non-recyclable plastic bottlecaps! These free materials, when re-used into ingenious craft projects, are kept out of landfills and thus reduce pollution, which makes them a great lead-in for environmental science lessons- or just for fun! These wonderful ideas are versatile enough for use in classrooms, parties, summer camps, boy and girl scout troops, projects at home, and even senior citizen homes. Also included is the musical play "*The Bottle Cap Kids*" performed at Disney World, with words, sheet music, and instructions for the costume making: even the costumes are made of bottlecaps! Activities include *Bottlecap Barnyard*, *Bottlecap Band*, a calendar of seasonal bottlecap crafts, and a variety of other fun environmental crafts.

While You Are Expecting: Your Own Prenatal Classroom

F. Rene Van DeCarr M.C. & Marc Lehrer, M.D.
PAGES: 160 / ISBN: 0-89334-251-3
PRICE: $16.95

Featured on Oprah, Donahue, The Today Show, ABC Evening Magazine and in *Newsweek, Reader's Digest, Parenting, Harper's Bazaar, Baby Talk, Doctor, Your Health, Omni, Image* and *U.S.A. Today*, this revolutionary guide introduces exercises which allow both parents to communicate with their unborn baby. Also included are tips for stress reduction and how to provide an optimum prenatal environment for your baby. Easy-to-use, this internationnally recognized manual explains the stages of your baby's physical and mental growth, while concentrating on interactive exercises which result in the easy birth of a calm, intelligent child who has already formed strong, loving, and communicative bonds with his or her parents.

CALL TOLL FREE 1-800-874-8844 • IN GEORGIA (404) 874-2176 • FAX (404) 874-1976 • EMAIL: learning@humanicspub.com

Science, Math and Nutrition for Toddlers: Setting the Stage for Lifelong Skills
Rita Schrank
PAGES: 136 / ISBN: 0-89334-280-7
PRICE: $17.95 / AGES: 2-4

This exciting new activity guide successfully introduces science, math, and nutrition concepts to toddlers. The importance of laying a strong foundation of critical thinking skills is recognized in this book, which details the abilities learned and practiced with each exercise. Thorough explanations of the scientific, mathematic, or nutritional principles accompany each activity, so no outside research is necessary- it's all included for hassle-free lessons! Developmentally appropriate variations are also listed for reinforcing concepts while adding on to toddlers' knowledge. Each activity is categorized to facilitate integration with older groups. Includes a large annotated bibliography and huge resource list for teachers and homeschoolers.

Homespun Curriculum: A Developmentally Appropriate Activities Guide
Denise Theobald
PAGES: 230 / ISBN: 0-89334-258-0
PRICE: $24.95 / AGES: BIRTH-ELEMENTARY

This book contains complete lesson plans for home-schools or classrooms are fully laid out in this book.. Each subject activity is age-group integrated with developmentally appropriate adaptations for the skill levels of infants, to toddlers, to school-aged children. Activities focus on reinforcing and enhancing skills in reading, math, science, social studies, arts and crafts, music/ dramatics, nutrition, creative play, games, and seasonal activities. Also included are detailed instructions on organizing your teaching space into centers or stations, creating integrated lessons around themes, organizing your time, scheduling individual development objectives, and getting organized and creative. This massive resource guide will answer all possible questions, objectives, and needs.

A Primer on Adlerian Psychology: Behavior Management Techniques for Children at Home and in School
Alex L. Chew, Ed.D.
PAGES: 128 / ISBN: 0-89334-271-8
PRICE: $16.95

Adlerian psychology balances theory and practical application for easy use by counselors, teachers, and parents who need to understand and communicate effectively with young children. Children are perceived as individuals with the creative capacities to decide and choose according to their private logic. Some Adlerian concepts explained are: active, passive, constructive, and destructive behavior patterns, the four goals of misbehavior, punishment vs. logical consequences, and personality/life style development.
Alfred Adler, a contemporary of Freud and Jung, was among the first child psychologists and his innovative perceptions of a child's personality development remain timely.

CALL TOLL FREE 1-800-874-8844 • IN GEORGIA (404) 874-2176 • FAX (404) 874-1976 • EMAIL: learning@humanicspub.com

INFANT & TODDLER

Teaching Terrific Two's and Other Toddlers

Terry Graham, M.A., and Linda Camp
PAGES: 224 / ISBN: 0-89334-106-1
PRICE: $17.95 / AGE: 2

When two-year olds begin in nursery schools and day care centers, they need activities specially designed to expand their capabilities and interests. A Humanics best-seller, *Teaching Terrific Two's* is the absolute best in-depth, structured activity guide for this delightful but hard-to-reach age group. The activities which both teachers and children will enjoy develop self-image, listening, language, social growth, movement, science, math, and music awareness to keep a young toddler's mind as active as a toddler's body. Includes introductory sections covering basic and individual goals, classroom arrangement, scheduling, discipline, materials, parent involvement, and assessment. *Shape Walks, Mitten Week, Bunny May I?,* and many other activities make this book an incredible resource.

"An excellent source of practical ideas and activities... a delightful, useful and meaningful curriculum resource... new and refreshing, this book will be especially helpful for the paraprofessional teacher of two-year-olds." — Dimensions

"A great source book, and a definite must for all teachers of toddlers." — Early Childhood News

"An exciting new resource book for parents and teachers of young children, by one of this countrys most respected authors and educators." — Educational Dealer

Toddlers Learn By Doing: Toddler Activities and Parent/Teacher Activity Log

Rita Schrank
PAGES: 160 / ISBN: 0-89334-085-5
PRICE: $15.95 / AGES: 2-3

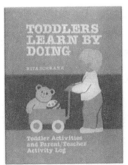

Your toddler needs a broad base of experience before starting preschool; the positive, fun experiences in this Humanics best-seller will enhance a toddler's enthusiasm for learning right from the start. This book includes activities for both active and quiet play, five-sense stimulation, language enhancement, concept development, and the fostering of independence. Old favorites are combined with new game, craft, and cooking ideas that use common, inexpensive materials. The activities within this book will help parents and teachers stay ahead of a toddler's short attention span and boundless energy.

The Infant and Toddler Handbook: Invitations for Optimum Development

Kathryn Castle, Ed.D.
PRICE: $16.95 / ISBN: 0-89334-190-8
PAGES: 128 / AGES: BIRTH-2

This Humanics best-seller covers every aspect of your new child's development, from birth to 2. Parents, teachers, day care personnel, education students- everyone finds this handbook indispensable. Developmentally sequenced by age group, this versatile book can be used as a materials guide in both formal and informal settings. Each activity is introduced by detailing the emerging ability and care giver role, while giving individual 'invitations' to care for and instruct these special developmental stages. Tips are included on how to introduce toys, store materials, develop basic care routines, create activity centers, and avoid trouble spots.

Pre-K Math: Concepts from Global Sources

Cynthia M. Manthey / PRICE: $16.95 / ISBN: 0-89334-240-8 / PAGES: 160 / AGES: 2-6

Finally, age-appropriate games, art, bookmaking, puppetry, fingerplays, and more to teach early math concepts to preschoolers. These creative, exciting, and engaging activities are refreshing alternatives to worksheets for teaching your children numbers. With these simple and inexpensive activities, children learn how to write and identify numerals, determine amounts through tactile and visual play, count from zero to ten and ten to zero, and do simple addition, subtraction, and estimation.

Each chapter focuses on a different number, so that each week you can concentrate on a new number while engaging a child's curiosity, sense of play, five senses, and interest. Pre-written letters to parents are included to encourage home involvement with the number of the week. There is also an overview of children's natural mathematical development, which explains the best methods of both teaching and learning. **Cynthia Manthey's** powerful combination of originality and variety are guaranteed to spark a child's imagination, curiosity, and interest in numbers.

SCIENCE

Science Activities: Leaves are Falling in Rainbows

Terry L. Graham, M.A., and Michael Knight, Ph.D.

PRICE: $16.95 / ISBN: 0-89334-045-6
PAGES: 192 / AGES: 3-8

The excitement and discovery of science exploration is introduced to young children with these thought-provoking activities. Successfully child-tested, these hands-on experiences help your children learn about science the way children learn best! Knowledge is gained, and retained, as children play with water, air, plants, magnets, and more. Activities extend from independent exploration to classroom projects. An excellent resource for the science learning center.

Energy: A Curriculum Guide

Carolyn Diener, Ph.D.

PRICE: $9.95 / ISBN: 0-89334-069-3
PAGES: 112 / AGES: 3-6

Energy is an extremely precious resource; we fight wars over the right to use it. Children can learn about its importance to everyday life, (and often take it for granted), where energy comes from, how we use it, and how to use it wisely, without destroying the environment. Activities involve mechanical energy, the human body, fossil fuels, solar energy, electricity, environmental responsibility, recycling, and energy conservation.

Science Air and Space: Folder Games for the Classroom

Jane A. Hodges-Caballero, Ph.D.

PRICE: $16.95 / ISBN: 0-89334-158-4
PAGES: 164 / AGES: 4-8

Science should be an integral, fun, hands-on part of daily classroom activity; often, however, it is not. This activity guide offers real life science activities which establish a strong foundation of scientific principles and concepts. The author distills her extensive scientific teaching background into easy-to-do activities in math, science, air and space travel, weather, women in space, and the environment. Includes resource lists and a preface by NASA Space Shuttle Pilot Colonel Gregory.

Hurricanes

Maria Gold, Ph.D. and Stephen Gold, Ph.D.

PRICE: $4.95 / ISBN: 0-89334-148-7
PAGES: 32 / AGES: 6-9

This introductory explanation of hurricanes is ideal for beginning science. Follow a hurricane's long journey from its conception off the coast of Africa to when it hits land. Weather symbols, maps of hurricanes paths, formation patterns, weather tracking systems, and safety measures give children a comprehensive education on hurricanes that will satisfy their curiosity and alleviate their fears of the unknown.

Can Piaget Cook?: Science Activities

May Anne Christenberry, Ph.D. & Barbara Stevens, Ed.D

PRICE: $14.95 / ISBN: 0-89334-078-2
PAGES: 130 / AGES: 3-6

Mix food with learning and cook up some fun! *Can Piaget Cook?* engages all five senses as it teaches about nutrition and the science behind the cooking process. As children measure and mix ingredients, they learn to follow directions carefully, as well as learning basic mathematical and scientific skills. Recipes for enjoyment include *Celery Coloring, Cheese Confetti, Rainbow Cake,* and *Vegetable Prints*. This innovative activity book involves inexpensive materials, so come and experiment in Piaget's kitchen!

Earthquakes

Maria Gold, Ph.D. and Stephen Gold, Ph.D.

PRICE:$4.95 / ISBN: 0-89334-155-X
PAGES: 32 / AGES: 6-9

Unpredictable, destructive, and frightening, yet an essential part of the earth's changing features- that is what earthquakes are. But how and why do they happen? This introductory science book explains earthquakes' origins, plate tectonics, seismology, volcanoes, and lava in a phenomenal beginning to earthquakes and geology. A glossary, safety tips, maps, and learning activities enhance students' vocabulary and language skills while teaching scientific fact.

CALL TOLL FREE 1-800-874-8844 • IN GEORGIA (404) 874-2176 • FAX (404) 874-1976 • EMAIL: learning@humanicspub.com

ACTIVITIES

Early Childhood Activities: A Treasury of Ideas from Worldwide Sources

Elaine Commins, M.Ed.
PRICE: $17.95 / ISBN: 0-89334-066-9
PAGES: 264 / AGE: 3-6

Over 700 child-tested activities, from a variety of teaching systems, are included in this overflowing encyclopedia of projects, games, and activities. Language and artistic skills, musical and physical awareness, and science and social studies are some of the subjects addressed. While dancing, singing, cutting, and pasting, the children will be so busy having fun, they won't realize they are learning!

Teddy Bears at School: An Activities Handbook for Teachers of Young Children

Arleen Steen, Ph.D. and Martha Lane, M.Ed.
PRICE: $17.95 / ISBN: 0-89334-092-8
PAGES: 224 / AGES: 4-7

Teddy Bears make every child feel comfortable in new surroundings. Friendly and easy to talk to, they are the perfect addition to the classroom. This delightful book fosters self-concept, language arts, math, and fine/gross motor skills. Includes an in-depth guide to designing and maintaining learning center activities for teachers on a limited budget. All the inspiration you need to create an entire curriculum of bear related activities.

Handbook of Learning Activities for Young Children

Jane A. Hodges-Caballero, Ph.D.
PRICE: $16.95 / ISBN: 0-89334-058-8
PAGES: 208 / AGES: 3-6

Designing innovative educational materials is no longer a chore with this handbook. Students and educators will be thrilled with these activities, which provide a guide to the creation of interesting educational materials. More than 125 enjoyable activities and projects focus on math, health and safety, play, puppetry, movement, science, social studies, art, language development, parental involvement, self discipline, and the development of a positive self-concept. This book is an especially valuable tool for CDA candidates since each activity has a stated purpose and a suggested functional area.

Art Projects for Young Children

Jane A. Hodges-Caballero
PRICE: $16.95 / ISBN: 0-89334-051-0
PAGES: 142 / AGES: 3-6

Developing a basic art program can be easy, even with a limited budget or time schedule. Over 100 stimulating projects that will improve motor skills are compiled here, along with detailed explanations of the various techniques necessary, from watercolors to batik. Activities are grouped into the basic areas of drawing, painting, cut-and-paste, as well as more sophisticated projects using textiles and photography.

Projects, Patterns, and Poems: for Early Education

Marion Ruppert, M.A.
PRICE: $17.95 / ISBN: 0-89334-108-8
PAGES: 175 / AGES: 4-7

Let children unleash their creativity with this wonderful collection of arts, crafts, projects, patterns, and poems for early education. The projects are grouped by the months of the year for easy reference to holiday celebrations. Full of clear and simple instructions, the Projects, Patterns, and Poems included have many variations for developmental adaptations. Delightful and informative, this resource guide is indispensable for the teachers, homeschoolers, and parents of small children.

Nursery Crafts

Jarie Lee Waterfall
PRICE: $17.95 / ISBN: 0-89334-107-X
PAGES: 224 / AGES: 2-4

These exciting new ideas for teachers, instructors, and parents are designed to help young children express themselves artistically. Successfully child tested, these activities involve easy-to-duplicate patterns and crafts that enable children to learn about texture, color, gluing, cutting, and identifying objects. While putting together these projects, children enlarge their learning capacity and memory skills, while experiencing a sense of personal achievement. Enable your children to construct their own mini masterpieces!

CALL TOLL FREE 1-800-874-8844 • IN GEORGIA (404) 874-2176 • FAX (404) 874-1976 • EMAIL: learning@humanicspub.com

ACTIVITIES

Scissor Sorcery: Cutting Activities for Early Childhood

Sharon Bryant Carpenter

PRICE: $16.95 / ISBN: 0-89334-076-6 / PAGES: 241 / AGES: 5-7

 Learning to use scissors is an important part of a child's education. Over 100 reproducible, fun activities teach children to cut safely. Developmental sequencing allows children to gradually improve their scissor mastery.

Child's Play: An Activities and Materials Handbook

Barbara Trencher, M.S.

PRICE: $16.95 / ISBN: 0-89334-003-0 / PAGES: 160 / AGES: 3-5

 Focus on the process, not the product of learning with this non-traditional curriculum guide. Used nationwide in CDA programs, it establishes positive experiences and sound relationships between adults and children.

Birthdays- A Celebration

Marilyn Atyeo, Ph.D., and Anna Uhde, Ph.D.

PRICE: $14.95 / ISBN: 0-89334-075-8 PAGES: 160

 Do you know someone who always throws spectacular parties that seem to involve no work or frustration? Chances are they have this book, packed with more than 200 practical and exciting games and activities to make a child's birthday into a magnificent celebration.

LET'S LEARN ABOUT.... *Best selling author and educator Elaine Commins has created five wonderful handbooks. Each book contains reproducible classroom exercises, student worksheets, posters, bulletin board activities, and special ideas for each subject area.* Elaine Commins, M.Ed. — PRICE: $4.95 EACH OR $19.95 FOR ALL FIVE / PAGES: 32 EACH / AGE: 3-6

Let's Learn About Language Arts
ISBN: 0-89334-147-9

Let's Learn About Math
ISBN: 0-89334-145-2

Let's Learn About Science
ISBN: 0-89334-143-6

Let's Learn About Art
ISBN: 0-89334-146-0

Let's Learn About Social Studies
ISBN: 0-89334-144-4

INTRODUCE CHILDREN TO THE FUN EXPLORATION OF BASIC SCHOLASTIC SKILLS.

Self-Esteem Activities: Giving Children from Birth to Six the Freedom to Grow

Angie Rose, Ph.D., and Lynn Weiss, Ph.D.

PRICE: $16.95 / ISBN: 0-89334-046-4 PAGES: 192 / AGES: 0-6

 Encourage children to recognize that they are special and unique, while understanding that their actions influence the feelings of others, that they hold responsibility for their behavior, and that no one can make them feel bad about themselves.

When I Grow Up : Volumes I and II

Michelle Kavanaugh, Ph.D.

ISBN: I: 0-89334-016-2 / II: 0-89334-017-0 PRICE: $14.95 EACH / PAGES: I: 206, II: 183 AGE: VOLUME I- 4-13, VOLUME II- 14-18

 Age appropriate activities to enable children to recognize and overcome discriminatory barriers. Sexual role/identity is highlighted for thoughtful discussion. Let your children reach their full potential.

Exploring Feelings

Susan Neuman, Ph.D. and Renee Panoff, Ph.D.

PRICE: $16.95 / ISBN: 0-89334-062-6 PAGES: 224 / AGES: 3-6

 Develop self-confidence, independence, and creative freedom in young children. These activities use everyday experiences for children to examine their feelings about their families, friends, and themselves.

CALL TOLL FREE 1-800-874-8844 • IN GEORGIA (404) 874-2176 • FAX (404) 874-1976 • EMAIL: learning@humanicspub.com

LANGUAGE ARTS

Drama and Music: Creative Activities for Young Children

Janet Rubin and Margaret Merrion
PRICE: $17.95 / ISBN: 0-89334-236-X
PAGES: 196 / AGES: 4-9

The reservoir of creativity inside you and your children is just waiting to be tapped! *Drama and Music* is a year round guide for incorporating constructive, educational creativity into your daily classroom routine.

The easy-to-read format is an invaluable tool for developing brief or extended lessons exploring music and drama while reinforcing other core subjects like math, science, and language arts. Includes background information on teaching and coaching, as well as activities, fingerplays, stories, and pantomime. An extensive index covers music, poetry, and literature. Make your class a dynamic, exciting place for integrated learning.

The Big Book of Folder Games: For the Innovative Classroom

Elaine Commins, M.Ed.
PRICE: $17.95 / ISBN: 113-4016
PAGES: 256 / AGES: 3-7

Games, puzzles, exercises, and projects stimulate primary students. This immense variety of file folder activities is specially designed to develop reading, mathematics, science, art, social studies and visual motor skills. Patterns, exercises, and worksheets are provided for easy teaching of these fun and simple activities.

Folder Game Festival:

Elaine Commins, M.Ed.
PRICE: $17.95 / ISBN: 0-89334-105-3
PAGES: 192 / AGES: 3-6

Hundreds of easy-to-make, fun-to-do games and projects using file folders are here. Each page is illustrated and includes simple preparation instructions and directions for classroom use. Reproducible companion worksheets and patterns are also included. Hand-eye coordination, pre-reading and reading skills, social studies, mathematics, and science are fostered by this invaluable resource for teachers, parents, and child care providers who need fun, educational, and easy activities for their children.

Vanilla Manila Folder Games

Jane A. Hodges-Caballero, Ph.D.
PRICE: $16.95 / ISBN: 0-89334-059-6
PAGES: 114 / AGES: 3-6

"Vanilla Folder" activities are easy to store and make, and they hold children's attention. The only materials needed are Manila file folders, marking pens, construction paper, scissors, and glue. The clearcut format of this book, which includes folders, patterns, and directions, will assist any educator in developing basic curriculum materials while staying within a limited budget. You'll discover the simplicity and fun that thousands of teachers already love.

Listening is a Way of Loving: Activities to Develop Listening Skills

Terry Lynne Graham, M.A.
PRICE: $16.95 / ISBN: 0-89334-156-8
PAGES: 176 / AGES: 3-6

Getting children to listen is a challenge for even the most seasoned professional. We prepare children for painting by dressing them in a painting smock. How do we prepare children for listening? The activities in this book teach sustainable listening skills, which are important long beyond childhood. Chapters include *Activities for Following Directions, Preparing for Listening, Whole Language- Whole Learning*, and *What Can Parents Do?* Teach children to participate in discussions, learn courtesy, and listen for main ideas. Create a loving link between parent and child with this essential resource guide.

Bloomin' Bulletin Boards

Elaine Commins, M.Ed.
PRICE: $14.95 / ISBN: 0-89334-113-4
PAGES: 160 / AGES: 4-8

Transform ordinary bulletin boards into hubs of activity! This guide will show you how bulletin boards can be used to stimulate active student participation and involvement. Exciting new ideas for art, science, math, social studies, language arts, health, and holidays provide provocative ideas that challenge children to think, do, and learn. Vitalize this valuable space in the classroom with patterns and ideas for backgrounds, clever captions, mounting, borders, and more.

LANGUAGE ARTS

The Flannel Board Storybook

Gloria Vaughn, Ed. S., and Frances S. Taylor, M.A.

PRICE: $17.95 / ISBN: 0-89334-093-6
PAGES: 192 / AGES: 3-7

Tell stories that capture everyone's attention using flannel boards! Simple, step-by-step instructions explain how to tell interesting stories, use the ready-made figure patterns, and create and utilize flannel boards and storyteller's aprons for all 22 stories. Developmental characteristics of children from infancy to middle childhood are highlighted to help you choose stories appropriate to a particular age group.

The Reading Resource Book: Parents and Beginning Reading

Mary Jett-Simpson

PRICE: $17.95 / ISBN: 0-89334-095-2
PAGES: 224 / AGES: 4-8

Everything you need to know about beginning reading instruction and language development is in this guide. A vast list of resources and a thorough evaluation of the different books available to young readers make this the ideal source guide for teachers, parents, and child care providers. Get your child started early with the interesting stories and fun activities in this book.

Fingerplays and Rhymes: For Always and Sometimes

Terry Lynne Graham, M.A.

PRICE: $16.95 / ISBN: 0-89334-083-9
PAGES: 160 / AGES: 2-5

Don't say it, sing it! Children will listen up quick, if you say it with a trick! Rhythm, imagery, and humorous nonsense will delight children while teaching them numbers, colors, shapes, self-concept, feelings, and more. This bestseller contains more than 250 original rhymes and fingerplays which help children learn through play, imitation, and repetition. Enhance vocabulary development, language skills, memory, hand-eye coordination, finger dexterity, and even attention spans! Rhyme and song in your lessons will make the ordinary exciting and new.

Storybook Classrooms: Using Children's Literature In the Learning Center

Karla Wendelin, Ph.D. and Jean Greenlaw, Ph.D.

PRICE: $16.95 / ISBN: 0-89334-043-X
PAGES: 224 / AGES: 4-8

Nurture your child's imagination with these activities. Children's literature come to life in a creative way with activities designed for independent use by children. Also includes ideas for creative expression in art, critical thinking, writing and drama, guidelines for organizing reading centers, suggestions for preparing games, and bibliographies for further reading. Entertain, delight, educate, and encourage a true love of reading.

Lessons from Mother Goose

Elaine Commins, M.Ed.

PRICE: $14.95 / ISBN: 0-89334-110-X
PAGES: 164 / AGES: 3-6

The colorful tales, historical lore, rhythmic cadence, and fantasy of nursery rhymes enrich the lives of young children while providing valuable learning experiences. You can introduce your child to the world of poetry, rhythm, rhyming, counting, and more. Each rhyme incorporates lessons in dramatics, language arts, math, art, music, and social studies. Let Mother Goose instruct a new generation.

"Great for educators working with kids and for parents who want to participate in the learning process with their children"
— The Book Reader

Can Mother Goose Come Down To Play?

Diane White, M.A.

PRICE: $14.95 / ISBN: 0-89334-136-3
PAGES: 144 / AGES: 3-6

Play is a child's best learning tool, and who better to teach the fun way but Mother Goose? Child and classroom tested, these projects improve sensory perceptions, language and social development, and science and math skills. These developmentally appropriate ideas include art projects, dramatic play ideas, and many other exercises to get children involved in the cheerful, fun world of Mother Goose.

CHILDREN'S BOOKS

The Adventures of Paz in the Land of Numbers

Miriam Bowden Illustrator: Anna-Maria Crum

PRICE: $10.95 / ISBN: 0-89334-150-9
PAGES: 32 / AGES: 4-7

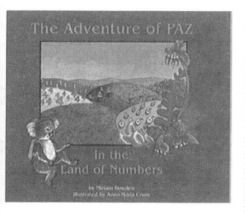

Venture into the Land of Numbers with Paz, the curious Koala, who discovers the magical inhabitants of this amazing land. Paz has never met the Pogo Sticks (ones), Unicycles (sixes), or the Trapeze Artists (nines) and he has difficulty recognizing them because they are all mixed up! Paz finds out that they are in need of help- they cannot get into their proper order. While Paz reorders the numbers, he masters them- in English and Spanish- and your children learn the numbers, too. Extraordinary illustrations surprise the reader with ingenious representations of the numbers 1 through 10.

"This joyous excursion through a land where numbers come alive will take the boredom out of learning to count for the very young"
— **Hilari Bell, Children's Librarian**

"This book allows the young reader to visualize numbers in a humorous and charming manner which stimulates creativity and makes for enjoyable learning." — **Jon D. Hammer**
Director of Continuing Education, Colorado Institute of Art

"Brimming with wisdom, this story leaves a child's imagination alive and pulsing."

— **The Book Reader**

The Planet of Dinosaurs

Dr. Barbara Carr, Illustrator: Alice Bear

PRICE: 10.95 / ISBN: 0-89334-161-4
PAGES: 32 / AGES: 4-7

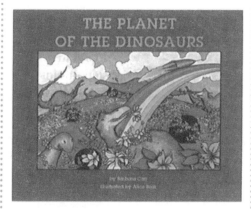

Could a dinosaur come live with you? Three young astronauts take a trip to the *Planet of the Dinosaurs*, where they find dinosaurs in need of a place to live. Explore the question of what it would be like to have dinosaurs live on earth again, and discover where the dinosaurs finally decide to live. Includes Whole Language reading tips from Dr. Carr.

Cambio Chameleon

Mauro Magellan

PRICE: $10.95 / ISBN: 0-89334-118-5
PAGES: 32 / AGES: 4-7

 Cambio is a chameleon who loves to change colors, but one day she loses this special ability. With help from her friends (several of whom are familiar from *Home at Last*), she learns a valuable lesson about appearances, feelings, and friendship. This endearing story has a strong message about self-esteem and the importance of drawing strength and happiness from within.

Home at Last

Mauro Magellan

PRICE: $10.95 / ISBN: 0-89334-119-3
PAGES: 32 / AGES: 4-7

Lego is a small worm with a big problem. The leaf that serves as his home (and occasional meal) is not a very sturdy home. So he sets out to find a new, better place to live. Along the way, he meets many different animal friends, who each have their own idea of the perfect home. This engaging children's story is beautifully written and illustrated by Mauro Magellan, drummer for the Georgia Satellites.

Max: The Apartment Cat

Mauro Magellan

PRICE: $10.95 / ISBN: 0-89334-117-7
PAGES: 32 / AGES: 4-7

 This heartwarming and inspirational story concerns a house cat. Max, who is cloistered in an apartment far above the hustle and bustle of the city streets outside. Max loves to watch the activity below his window, and one day decides to take a chance and venture out into the busy city world. What adventures he has!

"The pictures are very well drawn and quite engaging for the young child."
— **The Book Reader**

CALL TOLL FREE 1-800-874-8844 • IN GEORGIA (404) 874-2176 • FAX (404) 874-1976 • EMAIL: learning@humanicspub.com

Children's Books

THE FUN E. FRIENDS SERIES is ideal for beginning readers. Colorful, animated art filled with humorous details accompanies the text, providing amusement and a subtle learning experience for all readers.

Grub E. Dog

Al Newman; Illustrator: Jim Doody
PAPERBACK $3.95 / 0-89334-218-1
HARDCOVER $8.95 / 0-89334-214-9
Pages: 32 / AGES: 4-5

Grub E. Dog is very messy. He won't brush his teeth or comb his hair, and his room is filthy. Even his friends start to notice that he's stinky. Show young children and Grub E. Dog the importance of personal hygiene and cleanliness.

Giggle E. Goose

Al Newman; Illustrator: Jim Doody
PAPERBACK $3.95 / 0-89334-216-5
HARDCOVER $8.95 / 0-89334-212-2
Pages: 32 / AGES: 4-5

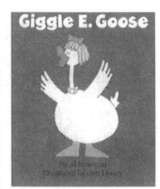

Giggle E. Goose doesn't know when to be quiet. She giggles in class, she giggles in the library, she even giggles and talks during movies! Giggle E. Goose needs to be more considerate of others. The young reader, along with Giggle E. Goose, learns that there is a time for giggling and a time for listening quietly.

Fraid E. Cat

Al Newman; Illustrator: Jim Doody
PAPERBACK $3.95 / 0-89334-219-X
HARDCOVER $8.95 / 0-89334-215-7
Pages: 32 / AGES: 4-5

Fraid E. Cat is afraid of the dark. She is so scared that she doesn't want to go to sleep at night. The chairs always seem to turn into bears, and her wagon turns into a big dragon. Afraid of what might be under the bed, this cat needs the night light on! A fun opportunity to show Fraid E. Cat and your child that there is nothing to fear in the dark.

Fibber E. Frog

Al Newman; Illustrator: Jim Doody
PAPERBACK $3.95 / 0-89334-217-3
HARDCOVER $8.95 / 0-89334-213-0
Pages: 32 / AGES: 4-5

Fibber E. Frog's lack of self-confidence leads him to tell tall tales to make himself feel better. No one takes him seriously anymore because he tells so many fibs. When you teach Fibber E. Frog to be happy with himself, your child will learn the same lesson.

CALL TOLL FREE 1-800-874-8844 • IN GEORGIA (404) 874-2176 • FAX (404) 874-1976 • EMAIL: learning@humanicspub.com

ASSESSMENT & TESTING

Humanics National Infant & Toddler Assessment Handbook

ASSESSMENT HANDBOOK (0-3) $15.95
CD-505A ASSESSMENT FORMS PKG OF 25. $29.95
SS-200 SPECIMEN SET (HANDBOOK & 5 FORMS) $22.95

Humanics National Child Assessment Scale Ages 6-9

CD-505-C PKG OF 25. $29.95

Student Motivation Diagnostic Questionnaire

Kenneth Matthews Ed.D. and Darrin L. Brown, Ed.D.
0-89334-131-2. $29.95.
PKG OF 25 QUESTIONNAIRES

0-89334-132-0
$19.95. MANUAL.

Humanics National Preschool Assessment Handbook

ASSESSMENT HANDBOOK (3-6) $17.95
CD-505-B ASSESSMENT FORMS PKG OF 25. $29.95
SS-100 SPECIMEN SET (HANDBOOK & 5 FORMS) $24.95
CD-521 WALL CHART $4.95

Humanics National Child Care Inventory

PRESCHOOL & INFANT ASSESSMENT MANUAL.
0-89334-088-X $10.95

Individualized Educational Program- I.E.P.

CD-506. PKG OF 100. $29.95.

Children's Adaptive Behavior Scale Children's Adaptive Behavior Report

R. Kicklighter Ed.D. & Bert Richmond, Ed.D.
AGES 5-11

SS-400 CABS / $49.95. SPECIMEN SET (MANUAL, PICTURE BOOK, 25 TEST BOOKLETS)

0-89334-055-3 / $29.95.
CABS STUDENT TEST BOOKLET PKG OF 25

0-89334-030-8 / $29.95.
CABR TEST BOOKLET PKG OF 25

0-89334-141-X MANUAL $10.95

PICTURE BOOK $14.95

This direct assessment tool is quick and easy to administer and includes national normative data. This interview guide utilizes the insights and observations of parents. Use with the CABR assessment or independently.

ASSESSMENT & TESTING

The Lollipop Test: A Diagnostic Screening Test for School Readiness

Dr. Alexander Chew, Ed.D.

SS-300 SPECIMEN SET / $49.95,
(MANUAL, 7 STIMULUS CARDS, 25 BOOKLETS)

0-89334-101-0 / $14.95,
THE LOLLIPOP TEST MANUAL

0-89334-140-1 / $29.95,
PKG OF 25 TEST BOOKLETS

0-89334-139-8 / $10.95,
SET OF STIMULUS CARDS

THE LOLLIPOP MANUAL &
7 STIMULUS CARDS $25.50

ALSO AVAILABLE IN SPANISH

Everyone loves *Lollipop*! Based on the latest research in school readiness, this test easily and quickly measures a child's readiness, strengths and deficiencies. *Lollipop* is easy to administer (15-20 minutes) and children love its colorful format. This test helps identify children who need additional preparation before starting school or who have special problems calling for additional psycho-educational evaluation.

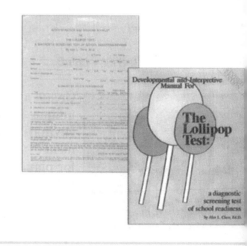

HUMANICS RECORD KEEPING SYSTEMS

HEALTH

Confidential Child Health Folder
(FOUR-PANELED FOLDER)
CD-512, PACKAGE OF 25 / $29.95

Confidential General Health Record
CD-513, PACKAGE OF 100 / $29.95

Screenings/Physical Examination/ Assessment Record
CD-514, PACKAGE OF 100 / $29.95

Confidential Immunization Record
CD-515, PACKAGE OF 100 / $29.95

Confidential Dental Health Record
CD-516, PKG OF 100 / $29.95

Child Nutrition Record
CD-517 PKG.100 / $29.95

Child Psychological and Social Development Record
CD-518, PKG. 100 / $29.95

Staff Observations of Health and Behavior
CD-519, PKG.100 / $29.95

SOCIAL SERVICE / PARENT INVOLVEMENT

Confidential Family Service Card Folder
CD-500 PKG OF 25 / $29.95

Confidential Home Visit/ Family Contact Record
CD-503, PKG OF 100 / $29.95

Parent Volunteer/ Inkind Record
CD-504, PKG OF 100 / $29.95

Recruitment and Enrollment Systems
SELECT OPTION A OR OPTION B
100 CHILD APPLICATION AND RECRUITMENT
FORMS & 100 CHILD ENROLLMENT REGIS-
TRATION FORMS / $59.95
OPTION A: FOR PROGRAMS WHICH SCREEN
APPLICANTS DUE TO LIMITED SPACE.
OPTION B: REGULAR

Confidential Child Application and Recruitment Form
CD-501-A PKG OF 100 / $29.95

Confidential Child Enrollment Registration Form
CD-502-A, PKG OF 100 / $29.95

Confidential Child Recruitment Record
CD-501-B, PKG. OF 100 / $29.95

Child Development Permit and Agreement Record
CD-502-B, PKG. OF 100 / $29.95

EDUCATION

Confidential Child's Activity Folder
CD-510, PKG OF 25 / $29.95

Teacher's Education Home Visit Guide
CD-511 PKG. OF 100 / $29.95

Let Humanics make your record keeping system easy — while complying with all state and federal requirements.

CENTER DESIGN & MANAGEMENT

Learning Environments for Children: A Developmental Approach to Shaping Activity Areas

Joan Sanoff, Ph.D. and Henry Sanoff, Ph.D.
PRICE: $12.95 / ISBN: 0-89334-065-0
PAGES: 104

Create a unique environment for play that promotes optimal learning opportunities. Now you can utilize the space and facilities you already have to design an area that will make your school or day care center efficient, pleasant, safe, and stress free. Organizational diagrams, playground planning, spatial layouts, equipment, psychological research, and activity analysis in order to help child care providers recognize the potential of each activity area.

Better Meetings: A Handbook for Trainers of Policy Councils and other Decision Making Groups

Carol E. Smith, M.S.W.
PRICE: $12.95 / ISBN: 0-89334-009-X
PAGES: 112

Meetings are an important and unavoidable components of any organization. meetings can either accomplish a little or a lot. With this handbook, your meetings will achieve all your goals- and more! The training programs and guidelines outlined here are for both group members and leaders. Find out how to foster enthusiasm and involvement while getting more accomplished.

POP: Planning Outdoor Play

Henry Sanoff, Ph.D., architect.
PRICE: $12.95 / ISBN: 0-89334-034-0
PAGES: 96

Why spend funds unnecessarily when you could easily construct your own unique, safe, and creative play area? *POP* provides all the needed information for building your own neighborhood or child care center playground. Find new ideas for incorporating learning areas and educational facilities into your site. *OPOP* can help turn a hard job into a fun-filled project!

The Administrator's Handbook for Child Care Providers

John W. Lorton, Ph.D. and Bertha L. Walley, Ph.D.
PRICE: $12.95 / ISBN: 0-89334-094-4
PAGES: 160

This is the most comprehensive handbook available for directors of early childhood programs. Staffing is an important factor of the quality of child care centers, but its overall efficiency is also a determining factor. Here's the definitive guide for organization, licensing standards, admission policies, financing and cost analysis, budgeting, equipment maintenance, staff selection, record keeping, child abuse responsibility, housing and space arrangement, morale, and more. Clear, thorough, and useful, this handbook is a necessity for any child-care provider.

Nuts and Bolts

Marilyn Segal, Ph.D. and Len Tomasillo
PRICE: $8.95 / ISBN:0-89334-063-4
PAGES: 78

A quality child care center is the product of intelligent planning and decision making. *Nuts and Bolts* will help you successfully set up an early childhood center, organize a classroom, write up an educational plan, and develop management techniques. Perfect for anyone setting up or improving a center, this book can also be used as a text for workshops and training.

CALL TOLL FREE 1-800-874-8844 • IN GEORGIA (404) 874-2176 • FAX (404) 874-1976 • EMAIL: learning@humanicspub.com

Organizing Parent Groups: A Model for Development of Parent Participation

Gary B. Wilson, M.A.
PRICE: $16.95 / ISBN: 0-89334-239-4
PAGES: 120

Parent involvement and participation seems hard to achieve, but *Organizing Parent Groups* presents an effective model that works. By implementing the systems and procedures in this guidebook, parents will be enabled to participate and make valuable contributions. This new system will help child care providers do a better job while involving parents in their children's education. Improve your school or child care program with the assistance of parents and the general community which is an achievable goal with *Organizing Parent Groups*.

Building Successful Parent -Teacher Partnerships

R. Eleanor Duff, Ph.D., et al.
PRICE: $9.95 / ISBN: 0-89334-053-7
PAGES: 84

Mutual understanding between parents and teachers is often difficult, but with the methods outlined in this book, cooperation can be achieved. *Building Successful Parent-Teacher Partnerships* deals with issues in parenting and teaching - the emergence of the two parent working family, the one parent family, and the disappearance of the extended family. By reading this book, which offers solutions to current problems, child-care providers and parents will learn, once again, to use constructive dialogue.

Activities for Parent Groups: Structured Developmental Activities for Parent Groups

Gary B. Wilson, M.A.
PRICE: $16.95 / ISBN: 0-89334-165-7
PAGES: 160

Tedious PTA meetings are a thing of the past! These motivating activities for parent groups will empower parents to play a vital, effective role in their community's child development program. The innovative, structured exercises facilitate teamwork within the child development program. Parents are instructed on how to understand and respect each other's viewpoints, formulate goals and objectives, and work together as an effective unit. Tips on decision making, conflict resolution, leadership skills, and meeting procedures will help any parent group become enjoyable and successful.

Lives of Families

Joseph Stevens Jr., Ph.D. and Barry L. Klein, Ph.D.
PRICE: $12.95 / ISBN: 0-89334-077-4
PAGES: 224

Discover a unique view of today's American families and the societal influences that shape them in *Lives of Families*. With articles written by scholars in the field of sociology, medicine, and education, this book includes moving discussions on the family, single parenting, issues faced by minority children, day care support, and other relevant topics.

Handbook For Involving Parents In Education

Doris K. Williams, Ph.D.
PRICE: $14.95 / ISBN: 0-89334-084-7
PAGES: 224

Get involved with your child's education by reading the *Handbook for Involving Parents In Education.* Everyone benefits from parental involvement in childrens' education, including teachers and administrators. Anyone concerned with the role parents play in the education and development of children should read this book. It contains the history of parental education, an overview of intervention models, and an excellent introduction to community support programs for parents. This book is a must for any parent that wants to play an integral role in the education of their child.

Parent Enrichment Trainer's Manual

Gary Wilson, M.A. and Tom McMurrain, Ph.D.
PRICE: $12.95 / ISBN: 0-89334-056-1
PAGES: 106

Everything you need to know in order to help parents establish closer, more meaningful relationships with their children is available in the *Parent Enrichment Trainer's Manual.* This manual contains materials for six structured training sessions (3 hrs. each) for new parent groups or refresher courses for existing parent groups. The manual uses techniques such as role playing, large and small group interaction, and journal keeping that are designed to enrich parent-child relationships.

CALL TOLL FREE 1-800-874-8844 • IN GEORGIA (404) 874-2176 • FAX (404) 874-1976 • EMAIL: learning@humanicspub.com